INTRIGUING INDIA
THE ALLURING
North

Wishing,

An 'alluring' long innings

TukluMama
Nov 2013

INTRIGUING INDIA
THE ALLURING *North*

Hugh and Colleen Gantzer

NIYOGI
BOOKS

Published by

NIYOGI BOOKS

D-78, Okhla Industrial Area, Phase-I
New Delhi-110 020, India

Tel: 91-11-26816301, 49327000
Fax: 91-11-26810483, 26813830

email: niyogibooks@gmail.com
www.niyogibooks.com

Text and Pictures ©: Hugh and Colleen Gantzer

Editor: Gita Rajan

Design: Write Media

ISBN: 978-81-920912-7-3

Year of Publication: 2011

Printed at: Niyogi Offset Pvt. Ltd., New Delhi, India

Contents

In the Nubra Valley, a village at the base of the Karakorams.

Preface

In the North, we followed their tracks through the high passes, their footprints left in legends and traditions, food, dress, festivals. Those wandering people, allured by the promise of India, filtered into our land, settled, and enriched the older foundations of our heritage. This is what drew us.

One of us was born in the East of our land, the other in the West. We had lived for many wonderful years in the South and have made our home in the highest mountains in the world, the Himalayas.

And so we started this voyage of discovery in the North. We followed the track of our ancestors through the tales in the *Mahabharata* and the *Ramayana*, the legends told in high temples snowbound and shut for much of the year, into caves and to a strange road where objects rolled uphill of their own volition. Always, we asked ourselves "How did it all start? What is the truth behind this strange happening, this intriguing custom? Why do these women kick food which they have cooked for their husbands, to their husbands? Why do men of a very patriarchal society allow themselves to be beaten by women in a public spectacle?"

These are just a few of the fascinating encounters we have experienced in our northern quest.

We know, now, that India is not a melting pot, as the US is. It is a mosaic. We have every racial group known to man, every ethnic mix, and every one of them has retained many aspects of the faiths and practices that were born out of necessity but still preserved because, in our land, the past has a sanctity of its own if it does not threaten the survival of the community. And, in India, we have 4,635 distinct ethnic communities.

We spoke about *their* tracks and *their* footprints. Who are *they*?

They live in your blood and ours and that of the people next door and ones at the far frontiers of our land. And even though some of us like to believe that we are ethnically distinct from others, the fact is that we Indians have more genes in common than any other people across the globe. We are a racial salmagundi, a smorgasbord of cultures, a wide-spectrum complexity of beliefs.

These are the bloodlines of living traditions that unify our rich diversity.

This is the India we have experienced, and write about. The India hiding behind the India you thought you knew.

Dark rocks with icicles hanging in crystal pendants, South Pullu.

The Lands Beyond the Mountains

NUBRA

We walked on the high plains of Central Asia, stood at the feet of the dark Karakorum Mountains, broke bread with the descendants of caravanners from Yarkhand and Kashgar. And yet we never left India.

Our friend Urgain Lundoop had said, "You've come so far. Why don't you come to my village in Nubra?"

"Where's Nubra?"

"It's behind the Himalayas."

Though we live in the Garhwal Himalayas, we'd never been to the back of the world's highest mountains. And so, with blue skies beaming over the capital of Ladakh we climbed into a 4x4 with Urgain and, at 12:15 pm, we left our hotel in Leh.

At 13:04 we saw tiny white pellets speckling the windscreen: it had begun to snow. We passed a place called South Pullu at 15,300 ft, and there were snowfields on the slopes. Icicles hung in crystal pendants on dark rocks and the wind had piled and sculpted the snow into bizarre creatures like bug-eyed goblins with tails wrapped around their heads. Our breaths steamed in the cold. Then, groaning and churning through the thick slush of the road, we reached Khardung La.

Festive strings of prayer flags fluttered above the snow-covered hillsides. A sign on a red board proclaimed: Khardung La, 18,300 ft. The Highest Motorable Road in the World.

The Army has become tourist-savvy: we bought a plate, commemorating the road, for the souvenir wall in our dining room. In their canteen we sipped

hot coffee and rubbed shoulders with mountain truckers who had leathery faces and raspy voices, faintly aromatic of diesel and sweat. One said he had seen a yeti on an earlier trip. The others chorused that they had heard that story before, many times, and hooted with laughter. When they tromped out, and we heard their trucks grind

The authors at the highest motorable road in the world.

To add to the eerie atmosphere, Urgain told us the tale of a monastery that had once held an evil goat-footed monster-monk who devoured little children. The distressed villagers revolted and burnt him alive in his ill-reputed sanctuary. It now stands as an abandoned and blackened ruin atop a lonely cliff, cursed and shunned by every human.

away, we asked the canteen man, "Have you seen a yeti, an Abominable Snowman?" He shook his head. "Not yet. But you say you're going to Nubra. That's at the back of the Himalayas facing the great, cold, plains of Tibet and Central Asia. There are a lot of stories about such things along that part of the Silk Road."

Along this branch of the historic road had come plodding caravans of double-humped Bactrian camels. As a boy, Urgain and his family had trudged up this frosty road carrying thick rotis, hard on the outside, soft inside. Now he was retracing his plodding trek in a 4x4, trying to persuade others to discover the austere and very beautiful land of his birth.

We drove out of Khardung La and started winding our way down into the valley. On the steep, frigid hillsides, where the wind had scoured away the snow, a black shaggy yak grazed on sparse grass. Its calf, with brown patches on its back, sought sustenance from between the rocks strewn across the

Left: Beyond the glint of the river rose the blueing back of the Himalayas.
Facing page: Stupas in the Nubra Valley.

slope. Our 4x4 clung to the Himalayan road and carried us deeper into the fold between the ranges.

And there, far below, was the Shyok River: braided ice-blue streams flowing across a platinum-grey bed with the cold neon-flare of the sun glaring behind the distant hills. If ever there was a setting for fearsome bearded trolls and crag-haunting hobgoblins…and, yes, yetis…this was it.

It became a shade warmer when we reached a village—willows bent in the breeze, a patchwork quilt of barley fields and vegetable gardens spread, flat-roofed houses staggered up the hillside. We spoke to bright-eyed schoolgirls and learnt from them that the medium of instruction in their village school was English with Urdu as the second language.

From the village we wound down to the die-straight road arrowing through the broad sandy bed of the Shyok River. Parts of the bed were covered with thick stretches of seabuck thorn from which people plucked the nutritious Leh Berry to be processed into an excellent fruit juice. This was also fodder for the Bactrian camels. There were herds of them still, in the Nubra Valley, we were told but we saw only one rather woebegone beast in a stone pen: the others had plodded away, somewhere, probably to the thorn thickets.

We stopped on the sandy bed and looked back. There, beyond the green fields of a village and the cold quicksilver glint of the river, rose the bluing backs of the Himalayas. We were now standing in the submontane slopes leading up to the awesome black range of the Karakorums.

This was a legendary, almost mythical-magical, land and we felt a frisson of excitement ripple over us.

A little later, still elated, we drove into Urgain's village of Tegar. The Yab Tso Hotel was a charming little double-storey building in the Ladakhi style with red plastic chairs and a colourful garden umbrella on the lawn. In the stillness and peace, the whisper of the distant river could have been the sibilance of invisible guardians hovering over us. It was a strange but oddly reassuring thought in this gently alien place.

A herd of pashmina goats at Panamik.

We slept very soundly at 10,000 ft and were woken by birdsong and the sun glistening on snow-capped peaks framed in poplar trees. Our breakfast of oven-fresh Ladakhi *nans* with honey and butter, cornflakes and sweet, hot, milky coffee fortified us. We were now ready to face a Nubra day.

A sign outside our hotel assured us that we were on the Silk Road. Before the high frontiers were closed in 1962, Trans-Himalayan traders would come plodding in. When the caravanners passed a spot that they felt was ill-omened, they threw a stone at it and these, in time, became chortens. Bell-shaped stupas grew out of them.

We passed one of these in its own, stone-walled, enclosure. It sat on a boulder platform and was roughly stupa-shaped and crowned by a green bush. It was a *Lhato*: a spirit who, occasionally, possesses one of his devotees and turns them into oracles. But if you don't respect it, it's likely to turn on you. Belief in such unseen beings is fairly common in wilderness all over the world: a natural human response to the implacable forces of nature.

Stupas also enshrine the relics of revered persons and protect wayfarers and natural resources. Not far from the hot spring of Panamik, four stupas, painted white, yellow, white again, and then blue, stood. They could have offered a reassurance to weary travellers along the Silk Road, or they could have been guardians of the thermal water bubbling out of the ground, offering a relaxing warm bath to people trudging down the caravan trail. Some of the water has now been fed into the PWD rest house, the rest flows down a rill, staining it yellow though, strangely, the mineral content in it does not have a sulphurous smell. It probably did, however, have an obnoxious taste. When we returned to the road, after touching the water in the yellow brooklet, a dense herd of long-haired goats with great, curving horns, and a few sheep, flowed past us. The soft pashmina wool, known as the expensive cashmere in the west, comes from the warm under-hair of these high-altitude goats so this herd was, in effect, a fortune in fabric-on-the-hoof!

There were about 200 animals being herded by Rinchen. A few of the lambs and kids scampered down to the rill and tasted the water and then jumped back shaking their heads in disgust. Rinchen said, "This is the first time they have come on this road. They will remember not to touch Panamik water again!" Obviously this is still a region where the seething fires of the earth have an effect on the surface: in fact, the great Himalayas are still rising at the rate at which a human fingernail grows, powered by internal pressures.

At the edge of a broad, green, soggy, plain a large outcrop of black, probably granite, rocks rose. Granite is a hard, crystalline, igneous rock formed in the deep furnaces of the earth. In the centre of this, was a pond called Lowan Tso, the Lake in a Rock, and, in all likelihood, it was filled with sweet water. But though we saw cattle grazing on the grassy, wetland, Pul Thang, plain that led up to this riverside outcrop, we did not see them drinking any water from the small stream that flowed through it. We then noticed that the meadow was dusted with a white, crystalline, powder. Urgain hurried down and returned with some of this substance. He said that they add it to their tea to give it colour and that, for years, his father had collected it for the government. They call it 'soda' so it could be a compound of sodium, blossoming like tiny mineral flowers on the surface of the bog.

Though dromedary caravans no longer plod in from Central Asia, the old Silk Road is still, very much, in use. A grandmother, mother and little son waited at the side of the road for a bus, the style of their garments showing the swift passage of history, and convention. Boulders carrying the beautifully chiselled mantra *Om Mane Padme Hum* reminded passers-by of their ancient eclectic faith. It had been brought to Kashmir and Ladakh by the greatly revered Indian Buddhist missionary Padmasambhava. Here it had merged with the spirit worshiping Bon faith to evolve into present-day Tibetan Buddhism.

A breeze from the valley brought the musky, overpowering, scent of the wild roses they call *skangba*. We broke off a tiny piece of it and saw a smiling woman looking at us. "We want to take it home to Mussoorie and plant it so that, in time, it will perfume our cottage in the Himalayas," we said self-consciously. Still smiling, she shook her head. "My daughter, she lives in Mussoorie, She has also tried; many times." Then she said something that encapsulated the hazards and rewards of our trip beautifully.

"If you want to breathe the perfume of Nubra," she said, softly, "then you must come to Nubra…"

The
Mystic Lake

A Naval colleague had first told us about Pangong.

'Ramu' Ramdas, as a hands-on Chief of the Naval Staff, had taken his team of divers to this deep, glacial, lake hidden at the far, northern, end of the high Himalayas. He'd said, "It's incredibly beautiful. You must go there…" Then he had thought a while and looked into the distance and added, "There's something about it that…" His voice had trailed away as if he was reluctant to express his feelings. As a CNS one has to be very circumspect about one's words.

And so we flew into Leh and decided to see things for ourselves. That's when we hit an obstacle. It had snowed the night before. The high road through the mountains was blocked.

But, as it often happens, our Guardian Angels worked tirelessly through the night.

When we woke at four in the morning, our hearts leapt. Snow still dusted the high peaks encircling Leh but the sun streamed down the road below our hotel. We asked our room boy what it would be like on the High Road through the mountains. The corners of his lips turned down, doubtfully.

Where mountains hold back icy terraced green fields spread.

"Pangong Tso is at 14,450 ft." In Ladakh heights are still marked in feet. "But you have to go over the mountains, through the 17,500 ft Changla Pass, to get there." He looked out of the window. A little later, hot coffee and biscuits, and a stalwart breakfast of pancakes and honey, decided it. We boarded our 4x4 taxi and headed for the 160 km long, winding, climbing, mountain, road.

A half-hour out of the valley we saw the first signs of snow. It dusted boulders and patches of hillside like icing sugar. Then, as we drove on, it became more assertive. It spread in furry rugs on the shadowy sides of the road, began to cushion the hillside, glistened in dangerous stretches of black ice. The slopes were covered with white blankets when we passed two laden trucks parked at the side of the road. Their crew called out.

"The army has closed Zingral. You cannot go beyond."

The trucks were right. The army camp at Zingral was a few metal-clad huts sticking out of featureless slopes of snow. A jawan told us that all traffic had to stop here: snow-slides had completely blocked the road ahead. Carefully…very carefully…we reversed and turned around, skidding a bit, and then tracked down the road again. We were very disappointed. Then we looked down on the right. There, below us, was an incredible eagle's eye view over a valley, meandering for 25 km between the lions' paws of the rising mountains. The terraced fields were stacked in tiers, each demarcated by its low, dry-stone, walls. The fields nearest us were green with young barley. Gradually, however, as the terraces rose higher, and deeper into the mountains, the summer green gave way to an autumn sere and then, winter frost glittered on them. Three seasons in a single valley on the same day!

It was irresistible. We turned right, down a snaking unpaved road, and into the Shakti Valley.

Stone walls protected the fields, grain dried on the flat roofs of the village, a winding flight of steps led through a gate to a curious monastery, the Tak Thog, built into a huge boulder. White scarves of honour were draped around golden idols on an altar under a golden canopy. Scrolls of the Buddhist scriptures reposed in rows of little alcoves behind. The old fragrance of incense and butter-lamps hung in the air like the reverberations of a bronze gong.

We left the ancient monastery and drove out of the Shakti Valley with a sense of *déjà vu*. We had been here before as children, sitting at a screening of *The Lost Horizon*: James Hilton's tale of a hidden valley in the Himalayas where time stood still.

But we still yearned to visit Pangong Tso. After four days of sunshine, the snow melted, and we set off again. We had spent those four evenings reading up on the legendary lake.

And Pangong is legendary. Shamanistic lamas use its shifting shades and flights of birds to predict forthcoming events. Then there is the oft-repeated story of the Monster of Pangong. We've pinned that down to the fact that

A camp of goat-herding nomads at 16,000 ft.

66 per cent of the lake is in Chinese territory and the Peoples' Liberation Army has been rumoured to surface near its lakeside hamlets, distribute goodies and pamphlets, and submerge again. Mini-submarines can easily be mistaken for marine monsters!

We left our hotel a little after dawn. The thaw had set in and the chortling gush of ice-melt streams filled the chill air. We crossed Zingral, soared upwards, stopped at the 17,800 ft Changla Pass. Here we drank coffee at the Border Roads' canteen with a family of visitors from Chandigarh. Then we crossed the snowy ridge of the mountains and began to descend. A herd of furry black yaks grazed on the stunted grass of a frigid meadow around an electric-blue lake fed by melting fields of snow. Below them was an encampment of yak herders. They are a friendly people whose shaggy beasts give them all they need: hair for their tents, leather for their shoes, milk, meat, butter and a fair income for their frugal needs such as borax for their *gur-gur* tea, tea leaves, parched barley and utensils. Their kitchen tent was woven out of yak hair; rough, coarse, brown-and-black, and reputedly waterproof. We were now at about 16,000 ft, which is as high as these Changpa, nomads, come. But though they share this rugged terrain with the goatherds, they claim to be a different people separated by centuries of

There were no oracles here, or monsters or other "ghoulies and ghosties". But there was certainly a Presence, that made a lasting impact on our minds and hearts. So, perhaps, it was rightly fated that we should not spend a night in the rather basic, but superbly situated, Resort Pangong Tso.

divergent customs and traditions. The tents of the goat-herding nomads were encircled by low walls of rocks, their long-haired goats finding sustenance in this arid land. Because of the cold, the goats grow a thick undercoat of fur-like hair, the valuable pashmina wool. We tried to get close but were warned off by snarling, amber-eyed dogs.

Now that we had learnt how to pick out life hidden in the scattered boulders, we began to spot other animals. Marmots, like fat brown terriers, squealed, sat up like begging dogs, and then vanished into their colonial burrows. Scurrying partridges looked like uniformed choristers recently embroiled in a fight: they had black circles around their eyes. We also flushed a pair of woolly hares nibbling on shoots of grass exposed by a melting rug of snow.

We were now at the wide, flat, bottom, of the valley and the great mountains had stepped back on both sides. A broad stream flowed slowly along its shallow bed and there were large stretches of sand eroded down from the treeless range. We spotted two four-legged equines grazing at the fan-like edge of one of these sand-slides, where it met the lush green of the flood-plain. At first the animals looked like horses from one of the encampments. But as we got closer we realised that they were kiangs: the rare Asiatic wild asses of Tibet. They had probably migrated down in quest of food. Later we were given another explanation by a Ladakhi guide. He felt that they could have been chased down into the valley by a prowling

Above: The many textures and colours of Pangong Tso.
Facing page: Tourists dwarfed by the great spread of Pangong Tso.

snow leopard who gave up the hunt because he would be conspicuous in this sandy terrain.

Then, as we climbed again, a cleft in the mountains opened, and we saw it. There, at long last, like a large glittering sapphire set in the claws of the Himalayas, shone the brilliant, blue, gem of the Pangong Lake.

We raced forward, drawn by its incredible beauty. It grew and grew, a coruscating crepe de chine stretch of cerulean blue, split by a sandbank thrusting a tarnished silver tongue into the lake. And, rising out of the far bank, were bare mountains of dusty grey and wood-ash crowned with capes of white snow.

It's difficult to describe the first impact that Pangong had on us. Or, for that matter, on others who have seen it and have spoken to us. It's hypnotic, magical, almost as if Pangong was alive and whispering a spell to captivate us. It was bewitching.

We drove closer and closer to its pebbly shores. Flocks of white gulls rose and wheeled over the water, their reflections causing ripples of light over the surface of the lake. But they were not the only birds in this high place. Bar-headed geese raised their necks and honked at us in alarm. Ruddy

A rare kiang could have been driven down by a snow leopard.

shelducks waddled out of the reedy banks and launched themselves into the water, quacking softly to encourage their ducklings to follow.

We stood for a long time at the edge of this magnetically beautiful sheet of water. Clouds drifted across the sky, making the lake seem as if its muscles were rippling, just below its skin. A starlit night on the shores of the lake, and the enchantment of dawn over those mysterious waters, would have cast an unbreakable spell over us: as it has over an Irish acquaintance of ours. He drives to Pangong whenever he can take time off from his job in another state.

Nevertheless, even though the tug of Pangong has been weakened over time and distance, we would still like to visit that incredibly alluring blue lake once again…

And once again, thank you Ramu. We know what you meant even though you didn't say it. There's something bewitching about Pangong.

When the Gods Stopped Dancing

THE DAHS

Our friend in Srinagar was convinced that he had found the descendants of Alexander the Great's army.

He said, "They're Aryans…definitely Aryans. Fair, sharp-featured and they wear tassels on their headgear just like the army of Alexander was said to have worn. In fact the Moguls adopted the tassel from Alexander and then the British and so did we. Our government orderlies still wear them on their turbans."

We had no idea what the soldiers of Alexander wore but his conviction that a remote tribe in the Himalayas could have descended from Alexander's army was intriguing.

"What do their legends say?" we asked.

He shook his head. "No one, as far as I know, has ever tried to get the legends of their origins. Dah is a remote village, difficult to reach."

Fascinated, we picked up our Inner Line Permits in Kargil and headed for the mysterious, Aryan, village of Dah. The mountains of Ladakh are unclothed, stark and very beautiful. The Indus is a foaming, silt-laden, river here, gushing and roaring through the naked mountains. We drove all morning on a road lying like a cobweb between the tumbling mountains and the snarling river. In the afternoon we stopped near a group of children waiting for a bus. Our guide asked them if they knew where the village of Dah was. "Oh yes," they said, "it's up that path."

Hardly a path—in places a Himalayan goat might have felt at home; in other places even the goat would have had second thoughts. We clambered over wet scree. Sometimes it gave underfoot and went tumbling down the hill and into the growling Indus. We tiptoed on as cautiously as cats on

A young woman from Dah with metal tassels on her head.

A man from Dah (left) with a typical Ladakhi male.

a crumbling wall. And then, after a long and tense trudge, the road gentled ahead of us. Trees began to overshadow it. A stone wall grew on one side. Fields spread their thick green quilts of barley. We saw women in bright costumes planting tomato seedlings. Children crunched raw turnips pulled out of the soft soil. A young man, in trousers and a short-sleeved shirt, came up to us and wished our guide in Urdu. He had sharp features and his eyes had no trace of the epicanthus folds on the eyes typical of many Ladakhis.

We explained that we had heard that there was a beautiful race of Aryans here and we had come a long distance to meet them and learn about their legends and customs. He smiled gravely and admitted that they were, indeed, Aryans and if we would follow him to the village he could find out more about their traditions.

The stone houses of their village were steep-walled in the Ladakhi fashion, but they also featured projecting eaves and balconies. There was a chorten-stupa under an apricot tree at the side of one of the narrow, single-person, lanes that wound through the village. As we walked through, people came down from their houses, friendly and inquisitive. Most of them had sharp features, all of them wore red shoklo flowers in their head-dresses: both the men and the women. The women also wore a remarkable amount of silver jewellery including silver tassels on their caps. The whole village was threaded with a complex system of covered irrigation canals: they crossed under roads, shot down channels cut into rocks, flowed down the sides of their extensive fields in a constant rippling murmur.

"Did you create this system all by yourselves?"

A burly old man in a sheepskin cloak said: "Our forefathers taught us when they came down from up there," he looked up the bare hillside to a peak, far, far, above us. Then, very graciously, he invited us into his house. It was dark and warm, dominated by a large, metal, stove. A rich, all-pervasive, aroma of melted butter hung in the air. We sat on benches and chairs covered in thick, fleece rugs.

"What are your legends? And where did your people come from?" we asked.

"Ah!" he thought a while. "According to our traditional songs, our first home lies far to the north-west. Our rivers and lakes began to dry so we had to think of leaving." He cleared his throat and said, "Our forefathers were led out of their stricken land by our mentors, the Lahs. But when they brought our elders over the high mountains, and showed us this land, it was bare. So our forefathers said that it was not suitable and they went back. But the next spring the Lahs led them here again. This time, however, our ancestors saw that, wherever they had stood the first time, green shoots of barley were springing up. They had used barley straw to line their shoes and, when they had dusted out their shoes, a few grains had fallen on the earth. Clearly, this was a fertile land. The Lahs and our ancestors then went back and brought our people here. Our mentors taught us how to tap snow-melt and bring it down from the high mountains, and make fields and orchards and houses. So, at first, we were very happy and thanked the Lahs."

He paused and a silver-haired woman came around with cups of butter tea which tasted a bit like soup. She then moved to a corner of the room and sat silently, a ray of sunlight touching the flower-buds in her cap, her eyes fixed on her grandson. Her face was deeply lined and very serene, filled with the wisdom of her years.

Our informant continued with his tale. "Yes, our ancestors were happy, but the Lahs were not. You see, they liked dancing and they had made a great dancing circle, ringed with stones, high in the mountains. And they came down and took away the best young men and women from the village and danced and danced and danced with them. So the work in the village was neglected. Then a great warrior of this village went up into the mountain and stopped the dancing. But the Lahs asked, 'Must our friendship break?' And the hero said, 'The work in the village must go on.' So the Lahs said, 'You work in the day. We will come visiting you in the night.'"

He stopped and nodded to himself for a long while as if deciding how he should word the rest of the legend. He cleared his throat awkwardly and said, "At that time we did not know how children were created. But one Lah used to ride into the village every night and visit a chosen person, as agreed, leaving before the first light came into the sky. It was also agreed that no one would ever talk about what they experienced with the visiting Lah, and no one ever did."

"Were the visiting Lahs both men and women?"

"Maybe. Perhaps. The songs do not say. But every night only one Lah came.

Two Dah women with their floral headgear.

Cheerful Dah women cultivate barley, vegetables and apricots.

That is certain. Then one night a childless old woman was overcome with curiosity. No Lah had ever visited her but one used to come to a young girl who lived in her house. So she polished the back of a pan till it shone and she hung it up on a rafter so she could see what they were doing. But since there wasn't enough light she held up a butter-lamp. But the girl saw it and screamed, 'Dawn has come! Dawn has come! Hurry! Hurry!' And the old woman also yelled, 'I have seen! I have seen!' And the Lah's horse pawed the ground and pawed the ground, impatient to bound away. And when the frightened Lah jumped on its back there was a bright flash like lightning, and a crash like terrible thunder, and a cloud of smoke and the Lah and his horse fled into the sky. And the hole that they left in the ground was so big that it took fourteen men fourteen days to fill it up. But after that, everything was all right." He nodded. "Yes. We did not need the Lahs. We had learnt how to do things for ourselves. And we did not have to go up into the dancing circle of stones in the mountains again. But it is there, it is still there." He thought for a while and added, "The air is very thin. I don't think you can climb that high in one day. Besides…" he paused. "…maybe the Lahs visit it sometimes. So it would be dangerous."

"Do you still worship the Lahs?"

"Maybe we never worshipped them. Maybe they were not our gods, only our leaders. But, you know…" he smiled knowingly, "when gods and leaders are no longer of any use, they are forgotten!"

All this, and his grandmother's story, was told to us long before the Kargil War. So, perhaps, the legends have been, largely, forgotten. Or maybe, the stone circle still stands up in the frosty mountains, where the air is very thin, and the zestful Lahs still fly in on their *vahanas*, flashing out of the high, cold, sky of Ladakh.

Town of
Strange Magnetism

Out of Delhi, high above the heat and dust of the summer-scorched plains, we soared.

Red-roofed hill-stations, stapled to the 2,000 m high 'foothills' of the greatest mountains of the world, appeared and receded under our flight-path, and still we rose. Glaciers of the great Inner Himalayas spread like goose-down on stark and frigid crests; ice-melt rivers snaked their way through cold valleys; conflicting cross-currents of air buffeted us like the invisible paws of capricious cats. The growl of our roaring jet engines changed, jagged ice-crags filled our windows, our descent began. We landed in the broad, mountain-encircled, valley of Leh.

According to the *Encyclopaedia Britannica*, "…at an elevation of 11,550 ft (3,520 m)…Leh is probably the highest permanently inhabited town in the world."

Elevation takes its toll. After the choking heat of the plains, Leh's air was chill, bracing and thin. We live at 2,000 m but, even so, we were advised to rest for a day to let our bodies get used to the additional 1,500 m. Everyone, in fact, must give themselves 24 hours to adjust if they want to avoid High

From the aircraft glaciers spread like goose-down on the higher Himalayas.

Tall poplars and spreading willows green the valley of Leh.

Legend has it that, another age ago, the villages around Pathar Sahib gurdwara were sorely troubled by a monster. That fearful, horned, creature had an insatiable appetite for human babies. The distraught peasants appealed to Guru Nanak Dev who was on a pilgrimage in Leh. When the monster realised that the powerful saint would foil him, the evil creature hurled a huge boulder at the Guru. Miraculously, the rock turned soft and, when it touched the saint, it took the impression of his contemplative body. Today, the imprinted rock generates an atmosphere of great, and lasting, reverence. The Army provides water for ritual ablutions and headscarves for those who wish to enter the shrine.

Altitude Sickness. We slept, read, watched IAF fighters take off, vanish over the snow peaks, land after keeping an eye on our neighbours across the high borders. The security forces are a constantly reassuring presence in Ladakh. Leh would have been cocooned in its protecting mountains if the Army had not built the world's highest motor-road through the 18,380 ft high Khardung La and 17,500 ft Changla Top passes. Nevertheless, Ladakh and Leh still deserve their old title: Great Thibet or Second Tibet. The terrain is the same, the flora and fauna are the same, and the customs and traditions of the people are still close to the ways of old Tibet.

We realised this when we drove up to the Peace Pagoda atop a hill overlooking Leh. At our feet spread the green valley of the capital, cupped by its naked hills. The infant Indus flowed through burgeoning barley fields, cattle grazed in meadows, and wetlands were dimpled with flotillas of ducks paddling over their own reflections blurring those of the mountains. We descended into the immaculately clean roads and winding lanes of this walking town: willows spread green over rushing, glacial, rills; poplars were verdant pillars; the old Leh Palace, squatting atop a bare crag, gazed over the valley town; and cliff-walled white monasteries rose with aloof, meditative, grandeur.

Buddhism permeates everything in the town. Gold-and-red prayer drums stand in decorated shrines at street corners. They contain thousands of inscribed invocations, and devotees who rotate them earn eternal merit by sending prayers swirling upwards. So do festoons of prayer flags and upright banners, though here the wind is the vector particularly when an afternoon dust storm rattles the panes and sends the windows slamming.

We drove out through flag-fluttering streets where bikers with shades made way for women from Amritsar whose families have been traders here for 20 years; folk from Mumbai shopped for carpets and pashmina, 'genuine fossil coral and amber', from shops that resembled a Wild West set with Ladakhi embellishments; and monks in strawberry robes, twirling prayers wheels, and mingling with foreign backpackers in fashionably tattered jeans. The carpets might be made in Punjab or UP, the 'coral' could be cleverly dyed stones, and that attractive amber pendant with petals and a scorpion encased within could be orange plastic with 21st century flowers and a dead insect. But then you'll find the same sort of tourist-trapping offerings wherever free-spending visitors congregate.

And so, in Leh, backpackers, with their chequered food habits, have spawned a wide range of culinary choices. We could have dined on Italian, Israeli and Greek fare, or even patronised a German Bakery.

Though Western backpackers are still a significant part of the Leh scene, they are being edged out by a growing new segment: affluent Indians in search of uncluttered destinations. The men, increasingly, opt to drive up in 4x4s via the rugged Manali route while their wives and sisters fly in. Those who enter Leh by road don't need to acclimatise their bodies.

We met some of these self-drive enthusiasts in the Pathar Sahib gurdwara managed by the Army. Here there is a rock bearing the impression of a figure bent in prayer.

Not far from Pathar Sahib is a hill. The Army has installed a board proclaiming it to be Magnetic Hill. We, and the Parliamentary Sub-Committee on the Official Language and their officials, in eleven cars, went to the bottom of what appears to be a rising road. We switched off the engines, put the clutches in neutral, released the brakes. And waited. Slowly, and then with increasing speed, the cars began to roll *up* the hill.

We tried it again and again, with exactly the same results. Then Samir Saran, a senior officer of the State Bank of India, laid a plastic bottle of mineral water at the bottom of the rising road. It, too, slowly rolled up the hill. Clearly, there was nothing magnetic about this phenomenon. But then what was it?

We were told that the impression that the road

The revered rock in Pathar Sahib.

A prayer drum stands at a roundabout in Leh town.

is rising is an illusion, brought about by the deceptive perspective of the surrounding hills. Possibly. But the hard-headed politicians and their equally cynical bureaucrats...and at least two travel writers...could have sworn that the road sloped steeply up a hill. And yet the cars and the plastic bottle rolled up it, unaided...over and over again!

Strange things can happen on the Roof of the World. And, in Leh, this one certainly did...

Mystical Powerhouses

THE MONASTERIES OF LADAKH

In the cold heights of Ladakh we went in search of the historical powerhouses that have sustained a deeply serene people, and their faith. Out of this has grown a resplendent heritage of art and culture.

We visited the monasteries of Ladakh in quest of such outward manifestations of a faith whose leader has won the Nobel Prize.

Our journey led us sixteen kilometres out of Leh to the Shey Palace and Monastery. It stood atop a rocky peak, as most of these monasteries do, looking down at a mirror-clear lake fringed by willows. In fact the word *shey* is derived from the Ladakhi word for 'mirror' and, we were told, oracles use the changing colours and images in the lake to predict future events. Such oracular pronouncements are a fairly common feature of Lamaism...the Tibetan form of Buddhism...and are also used to identify the reincarnations of revered teachers, like the Dalai Lama. Traditionally, the head lama of every monastery, or *gompa*, is a reincarnated soul. He is, consequently, deeply respected because of his reputed access to the wisdom of his earlier lives going back many centuries. In fact His Holiness the Dalai Lama is considered to have been reincarnated fourteen times.

One of the tests used in selecting a reincarnated monk is to place before a child, who conforms to the signs observed by the oracles, an assortment of objects including a few used by the earlier incarnation. The child must then pick out the ones which he had preferred in his last existence.

But it isn't only reincarnated monks who have a very special spiritual status in Ladakh, places also are revered. Shey is one of them.

The annual dance of the monks in the quadrangle of Hemis Monastery.

No person could rule as the King of Ladakh unless he had been born in Shey. It is a curious, but very revealing, fact of Ladakhi history, that the two-storey high gilt-bronze statue of the Buddha within the shrine was created by artisans brought from Nepal by the Muslim mother of a Buddhist king of Ladakh in the 17th century.

At the bottom of Shey hill, standing on the edge of the road, is a large rock. The images of the five Buddhas carved on it are the icons that devotees should hold in their minds when they meditate on the message of the Buddha. Such mental disciplines are not restricted to those who have renounced the world and have chosen a life of austerity and contemplation. They are also expected of lay persons leading a normal life in the world. Perhaps this is one explanation for the smiling serenity of most Ladakhis.

We moved on.

Nineteen kilometres along the flat river valley from Leh, rose the complex of steep-walled buildings of the monastery of Thiksey: stark and impressive in their beauty. The climb up to Thiksey is a strenuous one but the monastery made it all worthwhile. The gallery of its courtyard is bright with frescoes, all illustrating the rich folklore that Lamaism absorbed, largely, from its Bon roots. At the far end of the courtyard is a shrine built around a towering statue of the Buddha Maitreya: the 'Buddha-That-Is-To-Come'.

Above: Beyond the forecourt of Hemis rise the mountains with the cells of monks.
Facing page: The famed golden Buddha of Thiksey has a stylised ammonite in the middle of his forehead.

A monk clangs a cymbal for the dancers.

At the other end of the courtyard, and up a high flight of steps, is the oldest part of Thiksey. The monk on duty permitted us to go into the inner recesses of this shrine. There we saw dark images of the Mother Goddess bearing a strong resemblance to Himalayan deities predating the arrival of the Aryans into India. The old Bon religion of this land probably had strong links with the other nature-worshipping faiths that existed at that remote time.

Before we started trudging down to the base of the hill we looked beyond Thiksey. We were standing in old Eurasia. About one hundred and thirty million years ago the wedge-shaped subcontinent of India nudged against Eurasia, and, like the blade of a monstrous bulldozer, thrust up the bottom of the Tethys Sea, and created the Himalayas. The suture where the two continents collided became the green valley of the Indus, stretching away at our feet.

We drove across the flat plain of the Indus and into the bare and rising mountains where the famous monastery of Hemis lay hidden, tucked away in the poplars and the rocks.

Seventeenth century Hemis is best known for its great festival held in June-July. Tourists throng the gallery on one side of the huge courtyard facing the brightly painted four storeys of the monastery. In this central court, robed and masked monks dance to the measured beat of a wind and percussion orchestra. We had a preview of the festivities because the monks

One of the monks in the monastery told us that this great golden Buddha was a fairly new one and that this part of the monastery was built a decade or so ago. Even so, the powerful Third Eye of Illumination, in the centre of this image's forehead, has been shaped like an ammonite. This is an extinct mollusc which lived more than sixty-five million years ago in the warm Tethys Sea. Its fossils are often found in the rocks of the Himalayas because this area was once deep under the waters of the ancient Tethys.

were rehearsing their stately steps to the thud and blare of a small band. There is, however, a deeper and more meaningful aspect of Hemis.

We visited the four shrines of Hemis, each with a character quite distinct from the others. One housed the gold and silver images of Shamkhu Natha and the goddess Dolma also known as the goddess Tara. We got the feeling that both had a strong Indian connection. Here, too, there are interesting frescoes of the main events in the life of the Buddha and a fresco of a hermit poet identified by a monk as Milaraspa but also known as Milrapa. Before this seer started his mission he was said to have fasted for forty days and forty nights: exactly the period that Jesus did before He started His ministry. This similarity is interesting because some scholars believe that Jesus spent many years studying in Tibet before he returned to Palestine. According to Dr. Fida Hassnain, a Kashmiri scholar, Jesus was a student in Hemis which is reputed to have an enormous and ancient library of manuscripts. Years ago, when we met Dr. Hassnain, he told us that there is a statue of Jesus in this great monastery, but we could not identify it. Nevertheless, the legend of Jesus studying in India still persists.

Among the many shrines in Hemis is one dedicated to the great Indian missionary Padmasambhava. He vanquished the opponents of Buddhism by debate and example and became a hero of his people. The Hemis festival celebrates his birthday.

After Hemis, we decided to visit Alchi, reputedly it is the oldest standing monastery in Ladakh. Scholars say that the Ladakhi kingdom was established in the late 10th century AD. About AD 1600, however, the ruler of neighbouring Baltistan, Ali Mir, attacked and conquered Ladakh. An iconoclast, he plundered and destroyed the monasteries. Remote Alchi, near Saspol on the Srinagar-Leh highway, alone escaped destruction and its Indian-linked murals remained untouched. Consequently, it is generally believed that all of Ladakh's monasteries, except Alchi, date back no further than 1600. But though the monasteries were destroyed, their old books and records were secreted away and restored to the monasteries when they were rebuilt.

We found ancient Alchi unlike any of the other monasteries we had seen. Its wooden façade is carved in the Kashmiri manner and we spotted a modified *yali*-figure common in Hindu temples. We entered the main shrine called the Sum-tsek Temple. There are a number of subsidiary shrines with images of various Buddhas. Interestingly, in the Vairocana Temple, a profusion of frescoes covered the walls of the foyer of the main shrine. One of them showed a battle scene and, strangely, another showed boats.

Buddhism had been born in India and had been carried to Tibet by Indian missionaries. The monasteries of Tibet, asserting their authority, refused to allow Ladakh to open its own teaching centres. That cultural monopoly was broken after the Tibetan Empire fractured in AD 842 because of a conflict

Thiksey monastery gazes at the suture between India and Eurasia.

between the Buddhists and the followers of the old Bon religion, according to one historian. The Buddhists triumphed and they sent a young scholar, Rin-chen-zang-po, to study Buddhism in Kashmir, which was a Buddhist state then. This is known as the Second Spreading.

The carved woodwork and profusion of murals were certainly inspired by Indian motifs and, probably, were executed by Indian artists. Rin-chen-zang-po was only twelve when he went on his scholarly pilgrimage to India, but it was his influence that resulted in the unique architecture, and murals, of the epochal monastery of Alchi.

Taking the
High and Icy Road

CARAVAN THROUGH ZOJI–LA

For two days and a night we journeyed on a trail that was thousands of years old.

And yet it was brand new.

It took us through high, snowy, passes; past villages cut off from the world for seven months every year; over the towering Himalayan spine of a subcontinent; across the daunting Zanskar Range, and into the cold lands of Eurasia where the Indus flows, 3,500 m above sea level.

We boarded a jeep in Kashmir's lake-centred Srinagar where golden boats bobbed on their mirrored reflections and honeymooners were lost in their own fantasies of the future. The road wound out of the capital, past ancient chinars reputedly brought from Persia by the Mughals. Then we crossed saturnine Bakarwal herdsmen and their families. Trudging eight kilometres a day, leading and driving their enormous herds of goats and sheep, the Bakarwal men strode ahead.

Now the road began to climb into clear, alpine, country. The villages with pitched roofs gave way to the small homesteads of the Gujjars. They, too, were wandering herdsmen like the Bakarwals but now many of them have settled down and built their flat-roofed timber and earth houses, backed up against the slopes of the Himalayas. They cultivate maize and barley.

Ahead of us, the road rose higher into the mountains.

Trucks assemble in Sonamarg.

Now even the Gujjar huts were left behind and the terrain became more rugged. The mountain streams were angrier, growling and gushing around the boulders in their beds; there was a dusting of snow on the distant peaks. Unexpectedly, a green and undulating valley opened before us. It was ringed by snow-covered mountains; its meadows were dotted with sheep and grazing horses; its backdrop seemed painted: two Vs of dark mountains, one behind the other, and framed dramatically in the chevrons, a single, snow-covered, peak. When the sun caught it, it winked and coruscated like a brilliant diamond set in a primitive, cast-iron, crown.

Our road headed for that mountain and stopped short in a single-street hamlet. There were open-fronted shops on the left, rising green slopes and a few wooded cottages for tourists on the right.

We had travelled 85 km and Sonamarg, the Golden Meadow, was the start of our caravan trail into the jagged icy mountains.

"Will the road be opened tomorrow?" we asked the tourist officer. He was a dapper man in a grey suit and a smile of dazzling intensity. He looked up at the cloud-roiling mountains: "They say it will. They are preparing for it."

Sonamarg spreads 3,000 m high across a wide, undulating, meadow, ringed by mountains. Beyond a shanty tea stall, two hundred and fifty laden trucks were being marshalled in a huge field. The police sat in front of our barrack-like tourist hut, issuing permits to the truckers.

Later that evening, we spoke to the brisk, urbane, District Superintendent of Police in the flickering glow of an oil lamp. "We have to make certain that there are no breakdowns because they can endanger the entire convoy. We check the vehicles thoroughly; then we make sure that no vehicle is overloaded."

We also interviewed one of the truck drivers who would be behind us the next day.

Ghulam Nabi was a man of indeterminate age: early 30s by the resonance of his voice, late 40s by the bunched crow's feet at his eyes. "In the first convoy," he said, "we always take up bazaar goods: rice, dal, cooking oil, all the commodities needed for life." His voice rippled with an undercurrent of humour: the tough, confident, attitude of a man who takes his life in his hands every time he drives out to work.

It was raining when we closed the doors of our room. The rain pattered on the roof and the pressure lamp in the corner of the room hissed and smelt faintly of kerosene. Next morning the rain had gone.

We drove out of Sonamarg at 11:00 am and joined the other light vehicles at the barrier. The army vehicles would move out before us, the trucks would grind and snarl up behind. Balti men, like woodcuts from a Kipling tale, sat immobile against the backdrop of the high mountains. Their lined faces were expressionless, implacably patient. We looked away and saw Army signallers tuning their sets. Army officers looked at their watches.

A herd of goats cross a rock-hemmed glacier.

At exactly 01:00 pm, a colonel of the Military Police raised the barrier. The army vehicles drove through. On June 15, we became the first civilians, that year, to drive on the icy caravan road to the Zoji-La.

It was a journey we will never forget.

Traffic on the first 25 km of that mountain road—the most difficult part of the journey—moves in one-way convoys, very strictly controlled. In between the convoys, the men of the Border Roads Organisation work on the road: clearing away avalanches and rock-falls, draining ice-melt gushing across the road, towing away stalled vehicles, keeping constant watch and radio

Here, at Zoji-La, many historic years ago, a tough Indian Army General with the deceptive name of Sparrow had surprised his adversaries and routed them in the world's highest tank battle. The unforgiving weather of the Himalayas had obliterated the scars of that encounter but Sparrow and Zoji-La had earned for themselves an indelible place in the military histories of the world.

contact with others along the entire stretch of this miracle of a road: this ancient road made brand new every single day.

The winding road fled under our wheels, the bare hills blurring on the left, the sky wide and open on our right. The road clung to the side of the towering, wind-whipped, mountains. Here, the cliffs fell for thousands of feet and there was the sound of waterfalls roaring down. We were in a land of legends, in mountains burnished by myths.

The terrain changed. We began to be hemmed in by walls of impacted snow, gorges of translucent ice. Lonely yellow cenotaphs flashed past: little shrines dedicated to the courageous men who lost their lives building and maintaining this incredible road. The wind from the high peaks sang a harsh, shrill, threnody to their memories.

The mountains unfolded like origami sculptures: extending, growing with the speed of our passage. The cameos of the distant valleys caught in our throats abrasive with fear, excitement, ecstasy. We ground up a hairpin bend: *too sharp, too sharp!* We backed. Behind us the mountain fell a thousand dizzying feet below. Our wheels spun on the shale on the road, churned sickeningly; gripped. And we were around the bend, our traction hugging the road again. We released our breaths and smiled nervously.

Clouds were building up over the mountains, drifting down the ravines, spreading grey, deceptive mist over the road. A bulldozer, like a burly beetle, was grinding through a fallen hill, gears meshing. A man from the Border Roads Organisation controlled his mechanical behemoth with calm confidence, nudged the debris to the edge and over. We cheered and bumped across the landslide-hit road. On our left the mountains opened to a stretch of misty valley and icy peaks, and the neat, white, tents of the men who guard this road. No one sings ballads about them. No one remembers. An occasional white or yellow marker at the side of the road is their only tombstone. There are no flowers for them on this high, frigid, road. We left these sad little memorials behind: there was a daunting glare of white ahead.

We reached the snow line. The road had been sliced through walls of ice.

Rain pocked our windshield, thickened, became a blurring cellophane of flowing water. It was strangely warm in our vehicle but, before the windows were screened with moisture, we made out a road-sign:

"Zoji-La O"

We were 3,450 m above sea level.

Through the pass and down, we left the snow behind us and stopped at the military outpost of Gumri. A sign said: "Hold Your Breath. You are entering Ladakh". We were below the snow line: semi-wild horses galloped across the meadows of Minimarg, a herd of long-haired Pashmina goats drifted across a rock-strewn slope, their tiny hooves pitter-pattering like the raindrops that seldom fall in this high-altitude desert. Flowers bloomed in enormous and fragrant profusion, trying to cram an entire lifecycle into a few brief days of summer.

Buddhist chortens now began to appear at the sides of the road. In the distance the leafy streamers of willows fluttered in the wind blowing off the mountains. We glimpsed a spread of fields and a low cluster of flat-roofed stone houses. A little later we were in the single-street hamlet of Dras.

In June, Dras was warm with temperatures hovering at a benign 20 C or so. Men with wispy, white, beards and skull-caps sat in the sun; young men and women worked in the fields; children played in the dappled shadows of the willows. In winter, however, it is reputedly the coldest inhabited place outside of Siberia.

We paused just long enough in Dras to have a fortifying snack; then drove on past curious stone sculptures which were said to have been installed by the Emperor Ashoka, many centuries ago, and headed for Kargil.

In Dras, stone sculptures attributed to Emperor Ashoka.

Now we were in the incredibly beautiful mountains of Ladakh. Untouched by rain, unfurred by vegetation, the mountains of Ladakh were as naked as they were when they were thrust up from the bottom of the sea by the titanic joining of the subcontinent of India with the continent of Eurasia. They rose, ahead of us, in umber, russet, beige and orange. There were smoky grey, charcoal grey and blue-grey mountains and mountains as orange as tangerines. There were cliffs streaked with black, mountains striated like ribbon cake, and crags that looked like sand hills thrown up by giant ants. And always, holding up the indigo sky, were the crystal peaks of ice and snow. They fed the rills and the streams and the torrents and the rushing rivers, offering the only moisture that this highland receives, filling the air with all-pervasive susurration which is the theme music of Ladakh.

The light was fading fast and before we covered the remaining 54 km, we were in darkness and there was only the sound of rushing water around us. We spent the night in Kargil and slept well in this 2,750 m high hamlet.

Next morning, while the wind blew cotton from flowering trees, we looked across the gorge of the Suru River. A village clung to the mountains surrounded by orchards of apricots. Their soft-skinned fruit were as sweet and smoky-flavoured as fairy tales savoured in the log fires of memories. Willow and poplar and barley were massed green and inviting. A muezzin called the faithful to prayer from the mosque with the green dome on the main street.

Down in the bazaar, the shopkeepers were cleaning out their empty bins. The shops were bare. We spoke to Haji Ibrahim. "We have had no flour for one month but it will reach us within a week. You see, the road has been closed for seven months," he said as he continued to sweep out his store in anticipation of the provisions that the trucks would bring. The truck convoy was still grinding up behind us; it would reach Kargil in the night. We spent that day in Kargil, catching up on our notes, taking photographs while our jeep was being serviced. Shortly after breakfast the next day we strolled down the sunlit street again. The shops were filled with eggs, chickens, vegetables, grain. The convoy had arrived and replenished the winter-depleted larders of Kargil.

Our jeep looked bright, refreshed and revitalised. We set off on the last leg of our Himalayan journey to Leh, 231 rugged kilometres ahead. In places like Mulbek, however, the mountains stepped back to reveal a green and benign valley protected by cliffs that looked like eroded towers and battlements and bastions. Here stood the monolith of the Buddha Who-Is-To-Come: Maitreya. He seemed to spread his compassion, protection and serenity over the whole valley. Reluctantly we left this pleasant valley and began to ascend again, much higher than we had ever been on this trip. Even our rejuvenated jeep groaned and wheezed in the sparse, frigid, air.

A young trader in Kargil guarding goods brought in the caravan.

On the 3,700 m high Namika-La, The Pillar of the Sky, prayer flags were starched in the cold and we laid a stone of thanks on the chorten. We climbed higher and still higher to the 4,199 m Fatu-La. We were at a point higher than all the mountains of Britain and most of the mountains of Europe. The razor-sharp wind seared us and the slightest exercise in this depleted air made us pant. We felt a bit frayed around the edges. We had been on this road for more than 24 hours and we looked for some relief from these impossibly stark and beautiful mountains.

The monastery of Lamayuru was our heart-stopping reward, jolting us awake. It rose like the petrified flowers of the tortured rocks. Lamayuru is as heraldic as the set of a Wagnerian opera, a place of trolls and dragons and powerful wizards. There is a legend that, once upon a time, there was an enormous lake here filled with serpent people. The lake was drained by the founder of Lamayuru and all that is left of it are the pitted craters of a barren land, as alien and lifeless as the surface of the moon.

Oddly, however, geologists confirm that there was a lake here 30,000 years ago. How far back do the legend-enshrined memories of mankind go?

Now the painted mountains presented newer and newer perspectives as if they were turning while our vehicle crawled around the intricate serpentine loops of the road, dropping us 600 m to the bridge of the Wanla River.

The village of Khaltse was ahead, an obligatory tea stop, smiling people, prayer flags. Rice and a curry of boiled eggs and turnips tasted as delectable as the best gourmet fare. The long journey, the thin, cold air, had given us ravenous appetites. Leh lay 97 km ahead.

Fortified now, we felt that the road had become more gentle. It followed the flowing Indus, past Saspol, famous for its apricots. The fortress and temple of Basgho looked like a mad baron's castle in its eroded landscape of

A distant monastery outside Saspol.

red rocks. Beyond, there was a barren valley where prayer banners fluttered and dust billowed. The Indus meandered between green fields and, slowly, the patches of green increased and a distant hillock rose, crowned by Spituk monastery. It was still very far away and still very small, but it was very distinct because distances mean very little in this incredibly pure air.

Then the flat roofs of Leh appeared among spreading trees and, before we were quite aware of it, the bazaar of Leh, dominated by a ruined fort on a hill, was around us.

The world's most spectacular road journey had ended. We were a little stiff, a little tired: but very exhilarated…

When the Gods
Come Down From the Hills

DUSSHERA IN KULU

Once upon a time, we met a god.

We were driving on a road flanked by low stone walls, between orchards of gnarled apple trees, when our driver said, "There's a *devata* in front of us" and he sounded his horn and the god moved to one side. We drove ahead and stopped.

There were many people surrounding the god: men with close-fitting Himachali caps decorated with colourful bands; young women with full skirts, long blouses, jewellery and head-scarves; older women with warm, cloak-like, *pattu* robes also decorated with broad and colourful bands. "Generally," our guide said, "only men form the honour guards of the *devatas*, but this party had been delayed because the traffic had backed up, and so the women, who normally trail behind, have caught up with the men."

The god was idolised by gold and silver masks, draped in expensive robes, enshrined in a palanquin carried by the men. And the procession was preceded by drummers and heralds carrying long, curved, brass and silver trumpets to proclaim the arrival of the deity. Accompanying the god was his chief attendant, the head priest, the *pujari:* he carried the ceremonial silver sceptre of his divine office.

Crowds gather for the great Dusshera Fair.

The *pujari* said he was from the village of Jala and the deity was Ganesh Maharaj. "We have eight *dhole* drums and four *karnaili* trumpets," he said. And then he added proudly, "Though the rest of the *devatas* stay in the maidan, Ganesh Maharaj and his devotees are guests of the Maharaja."

Maharajas and Maharanis were, officially, dethroned many years ago in democratic India. But a large number of them are still enthroned in the hearts of their former subjects. You cannot dethrone tradition by fiat.

We drove in to the valley of Kulu after sunset. The great field to the right of the road was teeming with visitors and the enormous Dusshera Fair was in full swing. Cattle had been brought down from the villages and they were tethered to stakes next to their owners' campfires. There was a faint blue haze of smoke softening the scene wafting the resinous fragrance of conifer wood.

"My father had been a caravan trader with Tibet," an old resident had told us. He had looked around, recalling those distant days. "This was once a fair for horse traders from the highlands of Tibet and tea and cottage-craft traders journeying out from India." But the caravan trade had closed with the sealing of the border and now, in the distance, a circus had spread its tents and loudspeakers blared their repetitive music like a huge hurdy-gurdy gone berserk.

A light-spangled Ferris wheel moved slowly against the hazed moon, and great fortresses of brass and steel utensils glinted from the metal-smiths' stalls. On the main road, behind them, a canopy of tinsel shimmered in the breeze. This road had been converted into a pedestrian mall thronged with colourfully dressed people from the hills, the smart jeans-clad set from the town, and women from Lahaul in long, skirted, coats and tight churidar trousers looking rather austerely monastic in their dark clothes.

The brightest shops were those of the *halwais* offering rows of mouth-watering sweets in succulent tiers. Across the road from them were the stalls of the basket weavers and behind

Left: Himachali women in their festive finery.
Facing page: Drummers greet the mountain gods and goddesses.

them were piles of terracotta pots with finger wrought designs almost as old as those of Mohenjodaro. Finally, behind all the glitter and the razzmatazz of the fair were the tented camps of the gods and goddesses, lit by naked bulbs, guarded by their devotees, alert around their flickering camp fires.

Flowing through all this were great masses of moving, shopping, festive people.

No one really knows how many people come to the Dusshera fair. Estimates varied from a conservative civil-servant's assessment: "I would say that there are about 10,000 people milling around here this evening. But don't quote me. The police officials probably have higher figures."

They did. A police officer said: "Must be at least six lakhs."

"But," said a white bearded Sikh, sitting in his shop decorated with Himachali caps, "this year the fair is only four annas in the rupee," using an analogy drawn from the old currency of India. "That is, only one quarter of the people who used to come to the Dusshera Fair in previous years have come this year. Nowadays there are so many other distractions."

Nevertheless, the festival is still a delightfully eclectic mixture of the old and the new. On our way to the heart of the fair we strolled past the stalls of the itinerant dentists and opticians. "We also fix used teeth back in the mouth, sahib," a tooth-technician informed us cheerily. Then there were stalls displaying festoons of beads, bangles and brassieres... some of alarming contours...and rows of photographers' shops where it was the done thing to sit before a painted backdrop and look as grave as a condemned criminal.

The heart of the fair is the tented camp of Sri Raghunath Ji, the chief god. It is vast. Legend has it that three hundred years ago, the ruler of Kulu brought the idol of Sri Raghunath Ji from Ayodhya and installed this powerful deity as the lord of the Kulu valley. In order to ensure the paramountcy of his lord, the Raja decreed that all the other gods and goddesses would have to pay their homage to this great god every year at Dusshera. Since the Raja had been recognised as the regent of the idol, and he shared the great tent with his divine lord, he would also share in this homage!

Most of the *devatas* reach Kulu on the first day of the seven-day festival. It is only after the arrival of these lesser deities that the great goddess Hidamba Devi makes her appearance. None of the ceremonies can begin before this awesome lady is carried from her temple in a dark, towering, sacred deodar grove in Manali and installed in her camp in Kulu. It is only then that the idol of Raghunath Ji is brought from his temple near the Kulu Palace, down the winding, stepped, lanes of the old town, across the foaming Beas River, to the maidan.

The deities of Kulu have multiple metal faces, stacked in a pyramidal arrangement. The original face, the first to be consecrated, is invariably made of the sacred *panchaloha* alloy: gold, silver, copper, lead and iron. Then, depending on the power of the deity, and its ability to grant boons to its devotees, other masks are added below, all of them thanksgiving offerings of gold and silver. Little silver umbrellas protect some of the masks. And the whole array of masks is profusely garlanded in festoons of saffron marigolds and draped in rich, festive, garments.

We took time off the next day to visit the shrines in the hot-springs of Manikaran. When we returned, dust was rising in clouds in the turmeric light of sunset. We hurried to the great tent and stood near the flower-bedecked image of Raghunath Ji. The acrid scent of marigolds mingled with the fragrance of incense, the thudding of drums and the blare of trumpets produced an almost psychedelic aura, making our senses swirl.

The sun sank slowly. Expectancy built up. The beat of the drums and the haunting bellow of the trumpets grew louder and louder. The crowds started massing in front of the tents till there was just a sea of heads jostling and milling. The shadow of the hill crept across the maidan; came to the edge of the ravine of the Beas; paused as if it was hesitant; crossed the river and fell on the opposite bank. It was exactly 05:00 p.m.

And then the great *devata* durbar, the rituals of the Court of the Gods, began.

Drums thudding, trumpets blowing, cymbals clashing, devotees dancing, the gods and goddesses of Kulu came, swaying and bobbling above the surging crowds, intent on paying their homage to Sri Raghunath Ji. Priests prayed, gripped the palanquin poles, shivered in religious frenzy, conveyed their ecstasy to the palanquin bearers, and the awed devotees. "See! See!, the *devata* is alive!!" And indeed, the gold masks shimmered in the sunset light, the garlands swung, the palanquins

Roadside dentists ply their replacement trade.

The gods come swaying in their high thrones.

took on a compulsive vitality of their own: moving, rocking, trembling. Every *devata* was brought into the tent and placed, in obeisance, before Lord Raghunath Ji. And all the while drums pounded, cymbals crashed and trumpets roared stridently to the dust-clouded heavens.

After an hour or more of this we were drenched, limp, yet strangely charged as if something, vibrant with primal power, had surged through us.

And so, the next evening, when it was time to pull the holy chariot of Raghunath Ji, and thousands had massed again, we joined the jubilant crowd.

Sweating and straining at the great ropes, devotees tugged, knees bent, backs bowed, faces grimacing with the effort. Police held back worshippers and spectators from being crushed under those great, wooden, wheels. Slowly, the wheels began to turn over the uneven grounds. The crowd bellowed and cheered and clapped. The huge chariot moved, slowly at first, then faster and faster as the devotees shouted in triumph and called out to mighty Hanuman, the god of strength. Priests, standing on the chariot, guarding the idol of Ragunath Ji, urged the devotees to greater and still greater effort.

The chariot, creaking, reached the end of the field. Commands were shouted. The chariot stopped moving. The tired haulers, sweat pouring off their faces, staining their shirts, relaxed, breathed hard, flushed with triumph.

A ceremonial fire flared on the banks of the Beas, below.

Then, on the maidan, there was a great movement of men as the ropes were reversed and new positions taken.

Again there was a multi-throated roar as the devotees cried out and strained on their ropes. Slowly, the chariot moved back, up the slope, massive wheels turning. Inching, it crossed the length of the inclined maidan till it reached the camp of Raghunath Ji. The lord had returned to his temple home and it was time for the gods and their followers to go back to their villages for another year of toil.

We knew then where these people of the mountains had drawn their strength from. The crowd was the strength of the crowd, and their unshakable beliefs had fuelled them.

Dusshera in Kulu is not just a festival. Like many charismatic gatherings, it is an encounter with the deep wellsprings of faith.

The Vale of
Happy Solitude

KALPA

We came here, fleeing from connectivity.

We are standing, now, in a cedar-wood room, 2,860 m high in the Himalayas. There is a scent of resin in the air, the sound of flowing water, and, faintly, in the spangled starlight of this moonless night, snow-peaks glitter, rimming us with silver.

We are in Kalpa after an initially forbidding, tortuous, and very dramatic, journey. But we refused to be deterred, driven by a need to escape from land-lines and e-mails and letters and, yes, even from the ubiquitous and persistently invasive cell-phone. When we had asked a Himachali friend if he knew of a place where the connectivity is bad he thought we were out of our minds but then, very reluctantly, he said, "Probably Kalpa? Why? Do

Chini village and its orchards backed by soaring mountains.

The beautiful stone and wood homes of Chini village.

both of you want to take *sanyas*?" We nodded: "Something like that…for a short while…we're frazzled."

He shrugged. "If that's what you want, go to Kalpa. But get there as soon as you can. Three mobile companies are thinking of homing in. It won't be a *kalpa* for long." We didn't know what he meant but we took his advice and fled.

After the first, tenacity-testing, part of the road journey, things got much better. The terrain gentled, softened. Terraced fields began to spread, conifers marched like green regiments up the steep hillsides. The slim, silver-barked, *Chilghoza* pines held fat, emerald, candles of cones. Rows of bushy apple trees, laden with fruit, cosseted pretty, wooden, farmhouses with upper floors cantilevered out in the Kinnauri chalet manner. The cows wore bells, the women wore smiles and the men wore the handsome dignity of their Himalayan heritage with the assurance of mountain people in a blessed land.

Never have we experienced a place quite as contented as this.

And now, in the soft darkness of the starlight night, we will sleep peacefully. Tomorrow, we will explore this happy land in the lap of the Himalayas.

Soft dawn, and an insistent cuckoo, woke us. Light played over the mountains, touched the misted snow peaks, cascaded over cliffs and forests of deodar; spread gold over Kalpa. Fields and farms and orchards began to wake. An old woman climbed a rickety ladder to her flat-roofed cowshed, cleared it of grass and weeds, began to spread a mud-coloured plaster over it. The rising sun caught the grey, scale-like, slate roofs of Chini village on the escarpment beyond the valley and backed against the soaring mountains.

We planned to spend the day drifting around Kalpa. Drifting? Clearly, we have begun to respond to the unhurried heartbeat of this magical place.

We are back. It is almost sunset again and we have walked and walked and walked. But, strangely, we are not tired. We are glowing with the impressions which have filled us, today.

We strolled through the deodar woods, heady with the scent of conifer sap glowing like golden amber against the rough bark of the dark trees. Amber is the sap of trees fossilised millions of years ago. We pressed the petal of a tiny, snow-white, wild-flower into a tacky drop of deodar resin and wondered if we could write a story of that amber drop being worn by a distant descendant a million years in the future, in some remote stellar colony on the far fringes of our galaxy…

Flipping our minds back to the present, we trod gently on the carpet of soft, golden, needles threaded with walking paths. We found wild strawberries and larkspur bluer than the ones we grow in our garden, and hillsides covered with a grey-green herb as fragrant as a French perfume. We picked our way between rows of low beehives. We met two laughing girls filling water at a spring; a smiling man bent double and trudging under a sack of fodder; and a grandmother, her years etched gently on her face, feeding wool gently into a hand-held bobbin, while the sun made a halo of silver around her grey head. No one was in a hurry, no one frowned, everyone was steeped in serenity as if they had absorbed it with the air they breathed.

And perhaps they did; and perhaps we did, too.

Out of the deodar woods we walked, past a spring which fed a stream which flowed across a village road, cascaded down rocks and irrigated a field of seed pansies as bright as a floral carpet. Then we reached Chini village.

Chini's brilliantly decorated temple of Lord Vishnu.

A roughly cobbled street wound between wooden cottages with slate-tiled roofs. Little children played in front of their houses, old people sat warming themselves in the Himalayan sun, everyone else was at work.

At the end of the street a white stupa rose in front of a Buddhist temple. A woman walked round the temple and bowed to a Buddha enthroned on a brightly decorated altar behind a resplendent doorway. We walked on, and through a superbly carved door, entered the sunlit courtyard of a Durga temple. Golden lions and crocodiles guarded the ridges of the steeply-pitched gables; crouching gold lions stood menacingly near the doors; painted panels graced the intricately carved façade. The woman we had seen revering the Buddha now stood with joined hands before the Devi, praying fervently.

A warm feeling stirred within us.

At the lowest level of this shrine complex, down a flight of rough, stone steps there was a temple dedicated to Lord Vishnu. We heard a sound like castanets clapping and looked up. A fringe of wooden spindles dangled from the eaves, moving in the mountain breeze, slapping together. Below them, in the upward-turned corners of the slate-tiled roofs, bells hung, chiming musically. We have seen such decorations in East Asia and the first wind chimes in Japan were made of lengths of bamboo. Did the cultural roots of this small village in the Himalayas stretch so far across continents? The woman we had seen in the Buddhist and Devi temples walked forward daintily and prayed at the Vishnu temple. She then turned to us and asked, "Have you come from far away?" We said we had but that our home was also in the Himalayas. And then we asked a question: "Are you a Hindu or a Buddhist?" She smiled, turned towards the snow-covered mountains and did a deep namaste. And then she looked at us and asked: "What is the religion of the mountains?" Before we could answer, she was gone.

The warmth inside of us began to glow.

Walking up a steep path, winding between apple orchards, we entered the mansion of an affluent orchardist who had invited us to lunch. We drank butter-tea thickened with gram flour flavoured with almond oil. We spread *skand* sauce, made of the ground kernels of apricots and boiled turnip leaves, over the dosa-like *hoda* and *korashith*, which looks like a large brown *jalebi* and tastes like a *pakora*. And then there was the very powerful spirit called *rakh* distilled from apples and apricots and flavoured with a pinch of the world's most expensive spice, saffron.

Everything that we had eaten or drunk had come from this little valley. Ringed by the ramparts of heaven, it sat snug and contented, still independent of our frenzied outside world. But over the generations, subtle influences had reached in. We had heard about the fabulous costumes and jewellery worn by the brides of this area. It took a lot of cajoling to persuade a young woman to put on this traditional finery just for a photograph. It was worth the effort.

A bride with flowers on her head and a mask of silver filigree over her eyes.

The Kinnauri bride's hat, bedecked with flowers, bore a faint resemblance to the flat hat worn by the Tartars. The necklaces of silver, gold, turquoise and fossil coral had a Tibetan look. The designs in the woven shawl included the, so-called, Gordian Knot associated with Turkey and some Central Asian lands. But the silver mask and pendants flowing down like cascading locks must be unique to Kinnaur.

When she had gone, we sat down by our window and tried to collect our thoughts. Kalpa and the Kinner Kailash range spread beyond. The valley was settling into the dusk.

There are so many fascinating leads stretching out of this valley, so many hints of cultural strains, racial bloodlines, tapestries of varied faiths. These myriad influences flowed in here, over the centuries, entwined, merged and created the deceptively simple heritage of these people. We were tempted to unravel this brightly tangled skein and follow the strands to their distant origins. But we won't do that. Harmony cannot be shredded into its individual notes.

We have, however, got a message from the name of this beautiful place. Kalpa, as our Himachali friend must have known...and as we have now learnt...could have been derived from *Kalp vas*: Living in Solitude. Possibly, solitude has bred the self-reliance of the contented people of the valley, and their tolerance of the many streams of culture that have, very slowly, trickled in here giving them enough time to adjust. And perhaps...just perhaps...their generations of self-reliant, serene, solitude will sustain them through the pressures of the impatient future...

The Mystique
of the Timber Castle

NAGGAR

It was perched like an eagle's eyrie.

High above the Manali road, at the edge of a cliff, against the blue Himalayan sky, the castle sat. It looked forbidding, as castles should, clutching the secrets of its history in walls of grey stone and carved wood. But that was for the outside world, not for those who chose to live in it. For us, and the other guests, the HPTDC's Naggar Castle was warm and cosy, filled with the cosseting fragrance of deodar, the tree of the gods.

The main court of the castle.

We stepped out of our room and onto the cantilevered verandah. A faint breeze touched us and stirred the leaves of the apple trees in the silver-threaded valley of the Beas, 300 m below. According to legend, we were standing in a place where the Himalayan gods and goddesses had walked, when the world was young.

As they probably still do, in their own, cryptic way.

We strode out into the sunlit quadrangle of the castle. At the cliff-end of the lawn was the low, squat, slate-roofed shrine of the Jagti Pat Temple. Its *pujari*, Sharma, stood in front of the shrine and poured water from a pot raised high above his head. We took off our shoes and stepped closer to the shrine. An information board erected outside the temple said:

> *It was decided to make Naggar the celestial seat of all the gods of the world. They transformed themselves into honey bees endowed with Herculean powers and cut a slab from the Deotibba hill and flew it here. Even now, during any hour of calamity, all the gods of Kulu assemble here for the welfare of their people.*

When the priest saw us reading the board, he said, "Some people believe that this is how this place got its name. It could have been Deva Nagar: the City of the Gods. So that is why, if you look around, you will see so many

temples on these hills. It is a very holy place and people come here for its uplifting spiritual quality..." Incense burned on the black slab of rock in the shrine and bright flowers were spread over it. "Whenever I do puja, every morning and evening," the *pujari* continued, "the gods arrive." Just then, a honey bee landed on the door frame and flew in. "There," exclaimed the priest, "a god has just come to the temple! Others will follow...they are all around and they give great power to the stone."

The revered stone was also an oracle. It gives its answer after an

Pujari Sharma before the Jagti Pat Temple where the gods are bees.

The beautifully carved temple of Tripura Sundari.

*Among the legends associated with Naggar's long line of
ancient kings and queens is the one woven around a small
stone figure on a lawn of the castle. The legend says that
when rumours about the alleged infidelity of one of the queens
started circulating, the overwrought lady threw herself off a
high balcony. But before her body could touch the ground
below, it was turned into stone.*

overnight ritual involving rice, flowers and grass. The questioner has to decide which of these three offerings indicate "Yes", "No," and "Not yet" and then wait for a visiting bee to choose. If, in course of time, the oracle is found to have predicted correctly, then the questioner has to return to the temple within a year, and thank the stone in person.

Such mystic associations are part of the heritage of Naggar, the ancient capital of Kulu till about 1660. Legend has it that it had, earlier, been the principal town of this state for 1,400 years. When the rule of the rajas was abolished in Independent India, the castle was taken over by the state government and converted into a tourist bungalow. Great care was, however, taken to preserve its ambience and to ensure that it still remained a setting for the many legends that it had inherited from its former regal owners.

According to legend, the queen was sitting with her husband, gazing down at a wrestling match below. The king, spurred by an urge of overweening self-confidence, asked his spouse, "Who, in your opinion, is the handsomest man here?" To his dismay, and great humiliation, she pointed to one of the competitors: a well-built youth with sharp Himachali features and rippling muscles. In a fit of blind jealousy, the monarch bellowed, "Off with his head!" The match was stopped and the gory execution carried out immediately within sight of all the horrified spectators. The distraught queen shrieked and, fleeing from the royal balcony, flung herself over the cliff. But, as in the earlier legend, before her body could thud into the hillside below it was, miraculously, turned into stone.

Memorial stones seem to play a significant part in the lore of the castle. In its main court, where we dined in the dappled shade of a willow tree, there was a ring of stones, which were said to represent the old kings and queens who had once ruled from this high place. The custom of erecting such 'Hero stones', as they are often called, is fairly common in many parts of our land and the head-stones, installed on Christian graves, are probably a variation of this practice.

We strolled out of the castle and up a rising road. Here we came to the Tripura Sundari Devi temple. This was an exquisite example of the traditional stone-and-wood temples of Himachal. Its roofs rose in multiple tiers, the wood of its façade had been intricately carved, some with the sinuous figures of serpents worshipped by humans since the days of Early Man.

A more controversial, though even more fascinating, link had been proposed by the famed Russian expatriate explorer, mystic and folklorist, Professor Nikolay Roerich. The house where he lived, after coming to India with his family in 1929, is some distance beyond the Tripura Sundari Temple. To many it is almost a shrine permeated with the aura of those scholar-mystics. It holds a museum and art gallery devoted to the evocative paintings of the Roerichs, including those of his famous son.

Nikolay was born in St. Petersburg and made a name for himself as a scenic designer for the Russian Ballet. He was also an archaeologist and landscape painter. We know him best for his Himalayan works which go

The mansion where Nikolay Roerich searched for secrets.

far beyond representations of the mountains: they are evocations of the reality that lies beyond what the human eye can see. We always feel that if we look at these canvases for long enough we will perceive the hidden truths that these great mountains are said to hold, though that has never happened. Nikolay Roerich believed that many of the, so-called, myths of the Indian Himalayas and Tibet were true. He was convinced that the hidden city of the seers, Shambala, existed: possibly somewhere in Tibet. He also believed that the legendary, cure-all, herb Sanjivani still survived in the great mountains.

Roerich's most contentious conviction, however, was that Jesus of Nazareth had spent the fourteen "Hidden Years" of His life in the Himalayas, being groomed for His ministry by the great masters of Tibetan Buddhism. This is a belief held by many other scholars who contend that it accounts for the fact that Jesus preached a gentle creed of love, tolerance and forgiveness. To His Middle Eastern Jewish people, who believed in a vengeful and retributive God demanding 'An Eye for an Eye and a Tooth for a Tooth' Jesus asked His followers to 'Turn the Other Cheek,' and 'Do Good to Those Who Hate You'. Those who agree with Roerich contend that these were, essentially, gentle, Buddhist teachings and were thus condemned as heretical by orthodox Jews.

But though we always feel elated whenever we visit the Roerichs' home we cannot attribute any paranormal reason for these emotions. And we did not notice any divine bees buzzing around…

Looking for a Palace that Isn't

The ice-melt water of the stream was cold and sparkling on our bare feet.

We had stepped out for a picnic, in our drive from Mussoorie. And while we were munching our brunch, under a Himalayan oak tree, we re-read the *Mahabharata* translated by Rajaji. In the simple, lucid language that was his forte, he described how Duryodhana had plotted to kill Kunti and her sons. He had lured them to Varanavata on the pretext of having them join a great festival. Secretly, however, he had instructed his minister, Purochana, to have,

> ...a beautiful palace built for their reception. Combustible materials like jute, lac, ghee, oil and fat were used for the construction of the palace. The materials for the plastering of the walls were also inflammable...When the Pandavas had settled down in the wax house, the idea was to set fire to it at night when they were asleep.

The story is a familiar one and we have come here in pursuit of a persistent legend connected with it. It said that the Palace of Lac had been built in a village now called Lakhamandal. Naturally, there would be no trace of it now

because it had been set alight by the fleeing Pandavas. We felt, however, that we might, in our amateur way, be able to uncover a link with that famous conflagration.

It is time now to resume our journey up the hill to Lakhamandal and see things for ourselves.

It was a pleasant drive followed by a stimulating walk.

What a quaint and attractive village Lakhamandal is. There aren't many woods around the village, certainly

A lady of Lakhamandal in her carved balcony.

no forests, 'where the Pandavas used to go out hunting' and through which, 'Bhima strode effortlessly like a lordly elephant forcing his way through... pushing aside the shrubs and trees that obstructed his path.'

But after many centuries of human habitation, the forests have given way to terraced fields that stretch down the hillside like giant steps. There have, also, been more recent changes. A cemented path, winding up between parapets, led past a few *modern* concrete buildings. Beyond them, however, were the traditional timber houses of the village. We paused, enchanted by the sight of them.

Lakhamandal looked like a woodcut of a medieval European hamlet, except that these houses were much more beautiful. Their walls, pillars and arches were intricately carved. A man sat near his house using an adze to sculpt a handle for his bill-hook.

"Can you carve pillars and arches like those?" we asked.

He stopped his work, his face wrinkled in a smile. "Can you give me the deodar wood for such carvings? Can you persuade the Forest Department to let me fell a tree? If you can, I can carve!"

Uttarakhand takes its Forest Conservation Act very seriously. We looked around. Festoons of golden rope hung like blonde tresses from one of the balconies. It looked like bleached jute.

"What is that?" we questioned a woman framed in a carved arch.

"It is made from the Bhimal tree," she said. "We soak the young branches in water for six months. Then we strip the fibre and weave it into rope." She pointed to a woman carrying a load of slim, pale sticks on her head. "That's what is left after the fibre is stripped. They make excellent torches and burn for a long time."

Little pieces of a jigsaw puzzle began to fall into place.

We trudged up a long flight of stone steps to the highest point in the village. A Shiva temple stood there on one side of a large, stone-flagged, terrace.

"They say there was a large temple here; perhaps many temples," informed a bystander. "But they were destroyed...possibly in a fire...who knows?" He shrugged.

There could have been a large temple in the legendary town of Varanavata because, '...a great festival in honour of Shiva would be conducted with all pomp and splendour...' according to the scheming Purochana.

*To the right of the temple was a higher platform holding **shivlings**, and at the base of the platform were two stone figures. An interested bystander informed us that they were **dwarapalas**, guardian images that had been unearthed by the Archaeological Survey of India.*

We entered the temple. It had a number of seemingly old idols, greatly revered by devotees who streamed past. It was only when we were leaving that we noticed unusual symbols on the door. They had been beaten out of strips and sheets of brass and depicted a number of themes: a hunter with a bow and arrow shooting an antlered deer, people riding an elephant, two snakes, two women holding hands. The subjects were varied but the style was the same, and unusual. They had all been crafted in the manner of the Stone Age paintings we had seen in rock shelters in many parts of our land.

Our hearts began to thud a little faster than usual.

"Are these very old carvings?" we asked the *pujari*.

He shook his head. "No. They are not old. Some local people made them."

"Do they have any religious significance?"

"No. Nothing like that. They are only decorations for the door."

We peered closer. Some of them bore a distinct resemblance to the script of the Indo-Saraswati civilisation. We had visited both Lothal and Dholavira in Gujarat and had read a fair amount abut those ancient people. We were also aware of the opinion of a scholar who claimed that there was a strong similarity between that script and the still undeciphered Rongo Rongo script of the Easter Island people. Some of these symbols and petroglyphs, apparently, are akin to the early Brahmi script.

According to the *Encyclopaedia Britannica*, 'the Brahmi writing system...is ancestral to all Indian scripts except Kharosti...Among the many descendants of Brahmi are Devanagari...the Bengali and Gujarati scripts and those of the Dravidian languages...'

Though the brass embossings on the door of the Lakhamandal temple are comparatively new, they could have been copied and re-copied from earlier glyphs. It's possible that the earlier inscriptions were memorised and revered from those distant days when the first script came to, or was created, in our land. The names of the place also lend credence to this theory.

The Lac Palace was built in Varanavata. Local Sanskrit scholars have given us a whole bouquet of meanings for the word or words Varanavata, among them, 'The place to be remembered' and 'The place of the alphabet.' If either of these explanations is true, then the village we now know

The unusual temple door.

On the way to Lakhamandal.

as Lakhamandal, in searing memory of that terrible act of plotted arson, was earlier famed as the hamlet where the memory of the primal alphabet had been preserved. And not just as a memory, but as an actual record. In the temple in Chidambaram, in Tamil Nadu, the graceful poses of Bharatanatayam have been sculpted on its main door. Is it so difficult to believe that here, in Varanavata, far-seeing savants had preserved, for future generations, the greatly venerated letters of our first alphabet?

Or perhaps, as enthusiastic amateurs, we have been gravely misled. In which case, it was still a fascinating excursion out of Mussoorie.

Valley of the Brit Raja

He is a legend.

People still speak of 'Pahari' Wilson with a certain amount of awe shading into reverence. But, like all good legends, no one is quite sure of the facts. Was he a deserter from the army of the East India Company? Or an adventurer who had drifted into India as so many others had? Or was he the son of an English nabob and an Indian princess: a far more common occurrence than is generally believed. There is little doubt that he was either British or of British descent. And we, personally, are sure that he now lies, near his Indian wife, in a peaceful, conifer-covered Himalayan slope facing the distant mountains where his legend had been born.

And so one day, when autumn had spread balm over our wooded ranges, and leaves had begun to turn gold and crimson, we decided to drive out and discover things for ourselves.

On the winding, climbing, road, 25 km short of Gangotri, the conifers rise in serried ranks, like the green, guardian, armies of the high mountains. Buses, vans and cars wind through them, laden with pilgrims awed by the sight of the towering, white, peaks in whose melting snows the sacred rivers are born. We stopped to speak to a shepherd on this road, followed his pointing finger, and turned left into a narrow valley sculpted by two rivers and filled with the sound of their rushing, gushing, urgency.

A rare old portrait of the Wilsons.

Such river-wrought valleys are common in the Garhwal Himalayas. In fact the roads in this part of Uttarakhand often resemble the configuration of a switchback railway: soaring up to the chill bright heights of a ridge before plunging down to the humid banks of a river-valley. Harsil is such a valley and we spiralled our way a kilometre down from deodar forests to dense stands of willows; across a bridge; parked; hefted our luggage through an apple orchard and discovered the Tourist Bungalow of the Garhwal Mandal Vikas Nigam perched above the banks of the foaming Bhagirathi.

The narrow valley stretched to the right and left. Harsil looked very attractive that evening.

In the morning it was even more beautiful here, on the valley floor, than it was from the road high above. The sound of the rushing Bhagirathi, which waters the valley along with its tributary streams, is a constant backdrop to all conversations. The river rushes between white, pebbly, banks into the distant, blue, mountains which encircle Harsil. They are dark with conifers and rise to peaks: cold, crystalline and glittering with snow.

We picked our way along paths made of rounded stones, through orchards of old, gnarled, trees, across rustic, wooden, bridges, and into the single-street hamlet of Harsil. Trans-Himalayan travellers and traders had left their genes here. In the open-fronted shops, where men basked in the sun, we saw traces of sharp-featured Indo-Iranian ancestors, almost 'Red Indian' Tibetan implacability, round-cheeked Nepalese cheerfulness, and all the fascinating variations in between. Everyone was very helpful, directing us to the Wilson mansion and even beyond.

The double-storeyed mansion, built on a deodar-trunk frame filled with roughly dressed stones, was constructed like an old, European, trading factory. Massive stone gate-posts must once have held a formidable gate. The grounds of the mansion had been protected

Wilson's bungalow in the blue valley before it was destroyed in the fire.

by a high wall: most of it now recycled into the huts and *pushta*-retaining walls of the village. The ground floor of the mansion was functional and had probably held the storerooms, service areas and offices of Wilson's headquarters. We walked past sturdy door-posts which had held heavy doors, and into a passage between the rooms and extending to two more door-posts at the far end. In the centre of this protected passage, a flight of wooden steps led to the first floor.

The wooden treads were dusty but, even after more than a century, they were neither cracked nor did they creak.

This had, obviously, been the Wilsons' living floor, fronted by a broad verandah illuminated by peaked dormer windows. We made out a master bedroom at the far end, followed by a dining room and a drawing room, the stair landing, and three more bedrooms after that.

"Did Wilson have three children?" we asked the caretaker from the Forest Department.

He frowned for a moment, clearly unsure of himself. "That is what they say. My late grandfather was a kitchen boy in this palace of Raja Bhil-sen." He must have seen the expectant look on our faces because he hurriedly added "...that is what my grandfather said but by the time I met him he was very old and feeble and, perhaps, his memory was not so good..."

He followed us to the balcony that thrust out on top of the porch. "Here," he volunteered, "is where the Raja-sahib and his family had breakfast from March to October after the Raja-sahib had ridden around the valley and spoken to his headmen in the daftar hall below. From November to February, they had their meals in the *khana-kamra*..." He paused as if running out of steam.

"Did your grandfather tell you all this?" we asked.

He looked down for a moment, reluctant to meet our eyes. Then he admitted, "I was told this by some sahibs who came to make arrangements for the visit of Indira Gandhi. When she came to Harsil she stayed in the big bedroom at the end. She asked many questions and, sometimes, the babus around her would ask me to answer because I am from the village. They told me to remember everything because the Great Lady might ask me..."

We filed away his information as *generally unreliable sources* even though the descriptions he had given us made sense.

We wandered around and made a few discoveries for ourselves. All the bedrooms had attached bathrooms with doors leading to the service verandah at the back. Considering that, in Britain in Wilson's 19th century, a single bathroom served many bedrooms, 'Pahari' Wilson probably picked up his hygienic habits from Indians.

From the service verandah, at the back of the mansion, we looked down to the yard at the back. There, next to the wood-shed, and standing by itself, was a double-storeyed structure which was a mystery to the caretaker. We

A wooden cottage in Bagori village.

recalled a similar building we had seen in Scotland. It was a smoke-house used to cure meat and to preserve hides and furs. According to one legend, Wilson had started his life in the Himalayas as a trapper and fur-trader.

And then, to our delight, we discovered two old, framed, photographs in one of the bedrooms. They were of Wilson and his pretty Garhwali second wife, Gulabi. The caretaker seemed to be more confident when he said, "She was the niece of his first wife, who could not give him a child. Gulabi was the mother of all his children. Both wives came from the caste of drummers and they were from a nearby village."

Below the portrait of the bearded man was a caption:

F. Wilson. Pioneer, Forest Worker of Tehri Garhwal and
Builder of this Forest Rest House (1864)

In those distant days, when much of India was ruled by London-based traders, Wilson had settled here, planted an orchard of apple trees, and was, technically, a subject of the Raja of Tehri. But Tehri was very far away and so, soon, Wilson assumed the local title of Raja and even struck his own coins which were, really, tokens to be redeemed by his workers for British-Indian money in towns controlled by the East India Company. He had by that time, apparently, become a timber trader floating rafts of logs down the river to be converted into railway sleepers by the British.

Our visit to *The Valley of the Brit Raja* had been rewarding but we were still searching for more information about the legend of the Wilsons.

We left the old mansion and wandered on.

After a while, as happens in all *Lost Horizon* stories, we came to a village: a quaint, Himalayan, fairy-tale village. Prayer banners fluttered; children in heavy, woollen sweaters stood in the balcony of a double-storeyed wooden cottage, fascinated by us. The cottages had carved wooden facades, pillars and benches.

Cattle ruminated between piles of sawn wood and foraging chickens. A man in a woollen cap spun wool into yarn on a hand bobbin. A woman used a pedal-powered spinning wheel. Two girls wove a carpet on a hand-loom. There was a sense of contented permanence about this settlement as if it lived in complete harmony with nature and never found the need to change.

But this was deceptive.

These people, of Tibeto-Garhwali stock, migrate down to another village every winter. Bagori village remains shuttered, its street lifeless except for an occasional flurry of snow falling from a leaden sky.

We were walking back to the Tourist Bungalow, thoughtfully, when we met Dr. Nagendra Singh, Harsil's General Practitioner. Dr. Singh's grandfather had bought Wilson's general store on the shepherds' trail,

The old Wilson mansion with its fatal balcony.

running on one side of Wilson's mansion. We got talking to him and then asked, "What happened to the Wilsons?"

"Ah!" said Dr. Singh. "There were three sons: Charlie, Indrish and Nathu." Indrish and Nathu could have been the Garhwali diminutives of Andrew and Nathaniel. "The first two left and only Nathu stayed on. Nathu married two local girls from a village on the other side of the Bhagirathi, but he was too reckless to make money the way his father had. Instead he took to sitting on the balcony of the mansion with his gun. From there he would shoot the first sheep of every flock being driven to the summer and winter pastures, claiming these as toll tax for traversing his kingdom. Resenting this, the shepherds started driving their flocks early in the morning when the indolent Nathu was still asleep. When he got wind of this, Nathu was enraged. In his insane fury he shot the next thirteen religious pilgrims trudging past on their way to Gangotri."

"But," continued the doctor, "the Wilson name was so powerful in the valley that the Maharaja of Tehri could not find anyone to arrest this murderer. One morning, however, the villagers discovered Nathu asleep on a boulder near the river. They surrounded him, bound him, and carried him off to the Maharaja of Tehri. I don't know what happened to him after that...."

In just two generations the saga of the Wlsons had ended.

But there are some postscripts to this including one rather sad one.

The Wilson saga could have inspired Nobel Laureate Rudyard Kipling to write his famous story, *The Man Who Would Be King,* but the mansion built by the Brit Raja of Harsil no longer stands.

Some time after our visit, the Wilson mansion was gutted: destroyed in a raging fire accidentally started by a careless policeman.

Pahari Wilson and his wife Gulabi lie in adjacent graves in a conifer-whispering cemetery in Mussoorie. They had retired to this hill-station and, reputedly, built themselves a palatial mansion which they named after their eldest son Charles. In course of time it became a hotel and was known as The Charleville: the only hotel in the erstwhile British Empire in which British royalty has stayed. Queen Elizabeth II's grandmother, Queen Mary, was a guest in The Charleville, as the Princess of Wales, when her husband was shooting tigers in the forests of Dehra Dun.

Today, the former Charleville Hotel is the Lal Bahadur Shastri National Academy of Administration: the alma mater of IAS officers.

Thus by a quirk of history, Harsil is still ruled by the inheritors of the Wilson tradition...

The Wonders of a World Beneath

PATAL BHUBANESHWAR

Like Alice we vanished into a hole in the ground and emerged into a wondrous underworld...

Unlike the legendary schoolgirl, however, we had been here before and were not very keen to repeat our subterranean experience. But, at that time, we had written about it, and someone had read it, money had been given, and now things were not nearly so off-putting as they had been. In fact, *Pujari* Bhandari remembered us, thanked us, and said he'd send his son to show us the way into the sacred bowels of the earth. Bhandari had grown a little portly and prosperous over the years and he recalled, with a smile, how the way down had been slippery with moisture and the tacky soot of the smoky torches.

A visitor descends into the subterranean temple of Patal Bhubaneshwar.

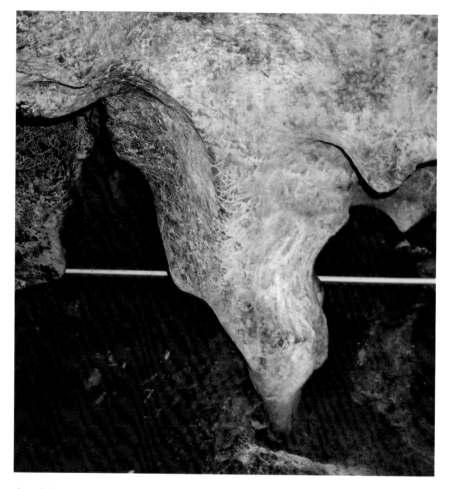

A rock formation revered as the hood of Sheshnag.

But now, Bhandari had assured us, things were different. They had a generator-set to illuminate the deep, underground, shrine, and chains had been installed for visitors to hold on to as they clambered down. That was comforting, but even more reassuring was the presence of his son: a young man who had probably descended and ascended through the pit a myriad times. He offered to accompany us into the depths of the earth.

Before we started our descent, however, he advised us to read the information board set up near the dark opening of the pit. We did. It proclaimed that: 'The Committee welcomes all Indian and foreign tourists as well'. Then it went on to assert: 'The cave was discovered by Ritupurna of the Sun dynasty in the Tritya era'.

Since that age goes back to prehistoric times this is, clearly, more legendary than factual. The board then stated:

'Chapter 103 of Manaskhand of Skand Purana [says that this temple was] consecrated by Guru Shankaracharya in Kaliyug. Since 1191, from the days of the Chand and Katyuri dynasty, worship has been going on. Only voluntary contributions are accepted to maintain the cave, temple, guide and oil expenses will be accepted — receipt will be issued by the temple committee.'

We made our contribution and then followed our priestly guide into the deep hole in the earth.

Those who are claustrophobic, and feel suffocated in enclosed spaces, should not attempt to enter Patal Bhubaneshwar. But though one of us did feel a little uneasy and had a tendency to hyperventilate, initially, this sense of panic stopped when we saw a man in a striped shirt, followed by two small children and their frail grandmother, climb up from the depths. They seemed quite elated. In fact the silver-haired woman said that she had had a very satisfying darshan of the many idols that no man could have made. "It's all a miracle!" she exclaimed. "Many miracles!" She smiled radiantly at us and continued her climbing-crawling way to the top.

We waited for her to leave and then continued down. Man-made steps had been chiselled out of the rock for a short distance, and there were no chains to hang onto. Our guide, seeing our uncertainty, advised us to sit on the steps and bump our way down. The white-veined, humped, black, rock had been worn smooth by the sliding seats of earlier pilgrims. Below it was another, smaller, white stone and it was from here...to our relief...that the chains started. Even so, it wasn't easy and, often, our guide had to place our feet on the toe-holds concealed in shadows. The supporting chains stopped at a spot where two rocks came close together with only enough room for a person to squeeze through and bend. We had to find whatever grip we could on rocks worn smooth by the hands of a myriad earlier pilgrims. "Clearly, the cave is testing our mettle before it lets us go any further," one of us remarked; and then we caught ourselves short, curbing our tendency to think of the shrine as a living, and slightly hostile, entity! After that it was a little easier: but only a little! The rocks had been cut into rough steps and we had to inch our way down them.

"See that indentation in the rock," said the guide. "That is the Pan Kund...shaped like a betel-nut leaf. Here Lord Shiva assembled all the nagas, and burnt them to ashes. But one escaped...that's the wavy black line on the rocks. The fleeing snake left that mark..."

Believed to be Lord Shiva's locks—a frozen cascade of filaments.

We paused now, and thought of the first people who had pioneered this descent. Holding spluttering, smoking, torches, they had not known what they might encounter in the stygian dark. That was a time when phantasms lurked behind every rock and chimeras gibbered in the night. Those ancient explorers must have been driven by an almost superhuman urge to challenge whatever lay ahead.

We resumed our careful plunge into the depths.

After we had descended for about ten metres...very cautiously, very slowly...into the earth, a cave opened in front of us. It was roughly bubble-shaped, with a diameter of about three-and-a-half metres, though it was difficult to assess heights and distances in the dimly-lit gloom of this underworld. Here, we met a group of people gazing around in awe as their guide pointed to a curious conglomeration of smooth, interlocking rocks. "There you see Ayravat, Lord Indra's great elephant!" An elderly couple did a namaste of reverence. Two teenagers flashed their mobile phones. A pre-teen boy said, "But doesn't Ayravat have more heads?" The guide smiled and said cryptically, "If Ayravat has more heads, then they are all there. If not, how can the rocks depict them?" The boy frowned and shook his head. The guide pointed to a group of small, conical, projections with their tips sliced off. "These are a thousand footprints made by some unknown deities, or perhaps by the Pandavas." The boy began to count them very assiduously till he was spoken to by a woman, probably his mother. He shrugged and turned away, grinning. He belonged to a younger, more sceptical, generation than the rest of his group.

We moved on and stopped at another rock formation at the far end of the bubble-cave. It projected up out of its rocky base and was shaped like the head of a cobra thrusting out of its raised hood. "Sheshnag," the guide said, identifying it as the immortal serpent, "And here, these lines on the rocks, are the marks of Sheshnag's backbone…" The boy piped up. "But how…" before his father put his finger on his lips and two couples, rapt and worshipful, frowned.

After that we had no interruptions. We allowed the flow of our guide's narrative to carry us along through the great river of tales and legends and beliefs that are part of the heritage of every Indian.

The cave narrowed and broadened, rose and fell, gave way to other caves and still others. The air was strangely cool and fresh. And the tales continued, pegged to the wondrous geologic formations as we followed our guide through this sacred wonderland. Up a slippery, undulating, path we came to Adi Ganesh and above him is the Hundred Petalled Lotus. "On the top of everyone's head is such a lotus so this is why the lotus has been shown and not the head of Lord Ganesh because the Lotus of Communication with the Absolute is more important than its container, the head!": an esoteric belief, common to all Indic faiths, woven into a cavern-guide's spiel. The iconic rocks assumed deeper meanings…Lord Shiva's locks were a frozen cascade of filaments: they were white though this virile Himalayan Lord has always been depicted with a thick, coiled, mass of raven-black hair. But that did not raise any queries from the pilgrims. They seemed to have suspended disbelief when they entered this awesome place!

Beyond, in the winding passages ahead, lay more revered images: The Kalpataru, the legendary Tree of Wishes, the fearsome open maw of Kal Bhairav, with its salivating tongue lolling out. "If you go through the mouth," our guide said, "you will not be reborn."

Coming up from the Patal Bhubaneshwar cave temple.

No one, apparently, was in quest of such instant nirvana. We trudged on, our shadows elongated and merging on the odd protrusions and contorted shapes of the rocks all around.

The voice of our guide streamed by us as we tried to visualise the titanic forces which had created this esoteric shrine. Patal Bhubaneshwar was a series of caves linked by a passage that had breached their dividing walls millennia ago. We were probably walking along the bed of a prehistoric river which had polished the rocks smooth but was unlikely to have given them their strange features. Those, in all likelihood, had been created by volcanic fires and twisting tectonic forces during the birth pangs of the earth. Then, after the hidden river had finished its job and vanished, the slow *drip-drip-drip!* of calcium carrying water had created stalactites of encrusted shapes, and the *splash-splash-splash!* of other drops had built up stalagmites rising from the floors of this dark labyrinth. All the five elements of the ancient seers... earth, air, fire, space and water had joined with the ethereal imaginations of mankind to create this enchanted shrine.

Our guide's voice brought us back to the present. We were in heart of the labyrinth: a small cave, about the height of a tall man and a little less wide. Here a natural *lingam* was encircled by a copper *yoni*. We paid our respects to these eternal emblems of creativity and when we were retracing our steps, our guide pointed to a small aperture in the right. "That was the passage through which Yudhishtra ascended into Heaven." He indicated another hole to the left. "The other Pandavas took this route..."

The world's two longest epics are ours: the *Mahabharata*, describing the war between the Pandavas and the Kauravas; and the *Ramayana* which relates the tale of the warrior prince Ram. They have both given rise to a vast panoply of stories, legends and myths that have enriched the graphic and performing arts of our land. Here, however, among all the profusion of icons in the depths of Patal Bhubaneshwar, there was not a single reference to any of the characters or incidents in the *Ramayana*. But we put aside that thought for another.

All over the world, all through time, the arts of man have tried to create images of the Other-world. Here, that work has been done by nature. And then we have endowed it with sublimity....

The
Source Seekers

We're not pilgrims, but this went far, far, beyond a pilgrimage.

We climbed, with thousands of devotees, high into the mountains of Uttarakhand. Our goal was to visit the reputed sources of two of the most sacred rivers in the world: the Yamuna, also known as the Jumna or the Jamuna; and the Ganga, otherwise called the Ganges.

We joined the stream of pilgrims in the beautiful village of Barkot. Surrounded by cathedral-like deodar forests, traditional timber houses with glinting slate roofs, gazed down at broad, wet, fields spreading back from the Yamuna River. Then, as we moved on, climbing higher and still higher, the mountains closed in, forming a gorge so steep that, often, the river was invisible in its dark depths.

Our fellow travellers, pilgrims and visitors drawn by the awesome Himalayas, flowed with us. Most of them stopped when we did at the first base camp of Hanuman Chatti.

The *chattis* are makeshift settlements that spring up on the mountain roads during the pilgrim season. Most of them are open-fronted shacks with wooden platforms for diners and sleepers. Piles of fat quilts rise in one corner and the cooking-fires are always lit, offering hot tea and vegetarian snacks and also rest for the old, infirm and weary.

We spoke to one of the tired trekkers. He was a tall, slim, man, clean-shaven with cropped white hair and a *choti*, a tuft, tied in a tight top-knot. He said he was a farmer from a rather impoverished village in Uttar Pradesh and was travelling alone.

A **chatti** *on the rugged pilgrim trail.*

The satin smooth coffee-toffee rocks of Gaurikund.

"Why have I come?" he repeated. "Why does anyone come? To make peace with The Mother. I have divided my lands among my three sons. My daughters are married. My wife is dead. Now I seek peace in the hereafter."

"But why have you chosen Yamunaji?"

He smiled revealing uneven, tobacco-stained teeth. "All my life Mother Yamuna has irrigated my fields. Who else would I choose? Eh?"

That was a very logical reason from a farmer. River-dependent agriculture continues to play a significant role in our burgeoning economy. We thanked him and moved on.

Hanuman Chatti's single street was crowded with people pouring out of their vehicles, or bustling into them, crowding into the shops, haggling with the owners of mules and horses because this was as far as the vehicles could go. Saddled horses, and *dandi*—palanquins carried by four sturdy hill-men, waited for custom. We chose ponies.

We had time now to notice the types of people milling around. There were young folk in jeans, some trying to jabber into mobile phones and looking very anguished because the high mountains cut off their connectivity; white-haired grandparents clutching bamboo staves; hawk-nosed men from the desert in yellow and pink turbans and luxuriant moustaches; mendicant sadhus in saffron robes, their faces and arms smeared with ash; the occasional trim trekker with a backpack.

We mounted our ponies very carefully. We hadn't ridden in years and expected the usual post-riding aches and pains. The road was densely wooded in parts, bare in others. Sometimes little rills crossed the road, trickling quicksilver from springs in moss-covered slopes. Beyond the rising slopes, there were sudden and dramatic views of the sculpted snow peaks of Banderpoonch.

A middle-aged man, muffed in a thick-knit sweater, windcheater, and a brown balaclava, stopped in front of us, turned around, smiled wearily and asked: "Excuse please... how you are not breathing hard, feeling the height?" We explained that we live in the mountains. His wife, bundled into a sari, green pullover, overcoat and with a mustard coloured scarf wrapped around her head and face, joined him, rested her hand on his shoulder and asked "Mountains? From Switzerland?" "No," we said, "from these Himalayas, the Garhwal Himalayas." They smiled a little hesitantly. "My name is Malik, Ash Malik. She is my missus, Mrs. Shanti Malik." His wife cut in: "We believe in the Great Mother. Yamuna Devi is an aspect of the Great Mother. And you see, we have a boon to ask. A great boon. So, if you want to be given a great boon you have to undergo great hardship. So that is why we have come...." We didn't catch the rest of her sentence because, just then, there was searing flash of lightning and a deafening crash of thunder. Mrs. Malik clapped her hands to her ears and exclaimed, *"Chalo! Chalo..."*

We began to regret that we had not taken a palanquin to protect our cameras.

According to our map, we had climbed from Barkot's 2,118 m height to Hanuman Chatti's 2,400 m elevation: just 400 m higher than our cottage in the oak woods. Ahead of us lay the 2,575 m high Janaki Chatti.

High, wooded, mountains rose in a V. And framed in the cleft were white peaks. At their base, but hidden from view, was Yamnotri.

Uttarkashi is, literally, 'The Northern Kashi'. A rather ominous belief is that, sometime in the future, the holy town of Kashi…which is another name for Varanasi…will be inundated in a great flood of water, never to recover. From then on, Uttarkashi will become the new Kashi.

The trek of 5 km from Janaki Chatti to Yamnotri was daunting and vertiginous. But, even so, we were accompanied by masses of pilgrims who didn't seem to be at all put off by the narrow, mountain-hugging, trail. We had decided to leave our ponies with their owner, in Janaki Chatti, and do the rest of the journey on foot. We hugged the hill side of the path not wanting to risk being nudged off the narrow track by a fractious mule. It was tiring and we wish we could say that it was worth the effort.

The temple to this important goddess was a very simple wood-and-stone structure. One reason for its unassuming appearance could be that it did not hold the source of the Yamuna. That, according to an official guide book: 'Lies about 1 km ahead and at an altitude of about 4,431 m. The approach is extremely difficult and pilgrims therefore offer puja at the temple.'

Before we could get to the end of the long queue of devotees, waiting to have a darshan of the idol, there was another blinding flash of lightning and rolling thunder which lasted for at least five minutes, reverberating from the hills. Steam billowing from thermal springs seemed to increase and the whole setting acquired a rather ominous aura about it. To add to our discomfiture, it began to drizzle slightly. We waited for it to stop and then hurried down to our waiting ponies in Janaki Chatti.

Some of the pilgrims were standing in a group, clapping their hands, tinkling finger-cymbals, ringing hand bells and singing the praises of Surya, the Sun God. When the group had completed its devotions to Surya, one of them smiled and then joined us when we were mixing the cocoa-powder we had carried, into glasses of hot, sweet, milk. We offered him some which he gratefully accepted saying, "One of the hardships of this trek is that you can't get anything but that awful *masala chai*." He told us that he worked for ISRO: the Indian Space Research Organisation.

We asked why he had made this pilgrimage. He smiled ruefully, thought a while and said, "Many of my colleagues have asked me the same question. I'll give you the same answer. The more technology spreads the more we realise that it is nothing compared with the forces of nature. Technology could not prevent the earthquake here, in Uttarkashi; or the increasing frequency of blizzards grounding international flights in hi-tech Europe." He paused. "So it is important for us to admit how puny we are. This pilgrimage is my admission of our insignificance in this universe."

But we still didn't know why they had sung the praises of Surya, and we forgot to ask him what the Sun God had to do with Yamuna.

Now, however, thanks to our friend and fellow author, Ganesh Saili, we know that Yamuna was the child of Surya and Sanjana, the daughter of Vishwakarma, the Chief Artisan of the Gods. But that marriage did not last because Sanjana could not take the continued radiance of the Sun. So her sister Chaaya (Shadow) took her place.

We believe that every legend is based on actual events. When the Indo-Iranians, who called themselves the Aryans, infiltrated into the northern plains of India, they were herdsmen. That was in the Bronze Age. "But," says noted historian Romila Thapar, "it is fairly clear that within the stretch of a few centuries, many communities began to use iron. It is also clear that with the coming of iron we have an unprecedented number of sites in the

Ice from melting streams feed the great rivers.

Ganga-Yamuna Doab…" It is likely that it was only when they came to the Yamuna that they changed from pastoralists to agriculturists. For this they had to fell the forests. This, in turn, gave them a ready supply of fuel-wood. They took to smelting iron in furnaces, the way that the Artisan of the Gods, Vishwakarma, did. The smoke of their forges darkened the sun like a Shadow.

Now we left the Yamnotri pilgrim trail and set off to follow other pilgrims heading for Gangotri, the town associated with the origin of the other great river: the Ganga.

We had to backtrack, pick up our car at Hanuman Chatti, drive down to Barkot, then on to the bend in the road a little before Dharasu, and finally take the left fork that would lead us to Uttarkashi.

It struck us, immediately, that there were more pilgrims heading to Gangotri than we'd encountered on the Yamnotri trail. One reason could be that the road to Gangotri is motorable all the way. Whatever the reason, the texture of the impressions flowing into us changed. The pilgrim trail to

The rocky road to Yamnotri.

Gangotri is rich in legends and we, and our fellow travellers, were regaled with them whenever we stopped and spoke to priests in the many shrines dotting this sacred route through the Garhwal Himalayas. It was like driving through a fabulous compendium of myth and legend.

The old and narrow streets of Uttarkashi do have something of the character of Varanasi. Here, as our ISRO acquaintance in Janaki Chatti had recalled, a powerful earthquake had devastated this town when the Himalayas had shrugged their shoulders. The great temple of the Lord of the Universe had, however, withstood that calamity. The pandit told us, proudly, that the unsculpted idol of Lord Vishwanath was larger than the one of the same name in Varanasi. He also told us that, here, two more tributaries flow into the Bhagirathi River; the Varun and the Asi.

Now, as we drove up the mountains, the wind caressed our faces and the river coursed below. A group of sadhus, sitting around a small fire, viewed us with mild curiosity. The town gave way to settlements, the settlements to fields.

We stopped at Gangnani, at an elevation of 1,856 m and climbed a flight of steps to a pool fed by a rill flowing from a small temple. Tendrils of steam rose from the pool. There was a slight, infernal, aroma of sulphur.

A mendicant with a grizzled beard and a complexion like a baby and piercing black eyes under beetling brows, said, "This is not the grandmother of the Ganga: it is not *Ganga-nani*. Please listen." His rudraksha beads rattled and rasped as he moved. "King Parashar said he could not defile the holy Bhagirathi by bathing in it. Maybe he found it too cold for comfort. Anyway…" he cleared his throat, "…so he prayed to the gods for better bathing facilities and they obliged. This is the geyser of the gods. The Bathing Ganga: the *Ganga Nahani*. Now go, have a bath. The sulphur is good for the skin."

The water was hot and it tingled. When we emerged we felt as if a skilled beautician had sand-papered our skins very gently. Our cheeks were as soft and as smooth as a baby's.

Millimetre by implacable millimetre, the Himalayas are still rising. Sometimes the sulphurous fires of their creation break through to the surface in hot-springs and foetid fumes.

We drove on, against the flow of the narrowing river. Temperate forests gave way to alpine ones. We shrugged into our anoraks and wound up the windows. Below us, the river wove watered silk patterns on the loom of its bed, flowing through the beautiful, and legendary, valley of Harsil.

The Himalayan terrain around us had gentled a bit, became more like the disciplined mountains of Switzerland rather than the young, rambunctious ones of Garhwal. Snowy peaks rose above dense woods of conifers. In sunlit terraces, cleared of the forest, fields were being ploughed by men in homespun tweed and sharp-featured women in bright headscarves, blouses and full skirts. And everywhere there was the sound of trickling, tinkling, gurgling, rushing water.

As we got closer to Gangotri, the folklore associated with shrines and events grew denser and denser. Legends wreathed around us when we stopped at the checkpost of Bhairon-Ghatti. A little shrine on a stone platform, bright with fluttering flags, was backed against a mass of conifers pressed to increasingly bare and eroded cliffs as they soared to the high, cloud-scudding, sky.

Bhairon, also known as Bhairav, is a terrifying figure with matted hair hanging in strands like banyan roots. He holds His Lord's trident as leader of Lord Shiva's goblin horde, a begging bowl made of a human skull, and ornaments fashioned like snakes. He also has a slim, whippet-like, dog which, according to some folks, points to his tribal origins. When we stood on the platform of the temple, with the wooded mountains hemming us in, the atmosphere was a little eerie.

A little later, we entered the teeming, milling, slightly chaotic outskirts of the pilgrim town of Gangotri. We honked, crawled, manoeuvred our car through colourful throngs of pilgrims; inveigled our way through increasingly irate crowds of people and, eventually, arrived at the Tourist Bungalow.

A little later we stepped out of our room and stood at 3,200 m on the craggy slopes above the 18th century town of Gangotri. Saffron-clad pilgrims dotted the pebbly banks of the river below, bathing in its chill waters. The clouds had cleared. And beyond, in the unseen distance, was the arch supporting the mass of ice and snow called Gaumukh. Here, part of the river is born in a gush of frigid water. Appropriately, it is called the Bhagirathi after the pious monarch of Ayodhya whose austerities, many believe, brought the river down from the skies.

Once upon a time, so the legend goes, King Bhagirath prayed for the descent of the Ganga from the heavens. He wanted its holy waters to give absolution to his clan who had been incinerated by the fury of a sage. But if the Ganga had descended in all her titanic fury, the world would have been inundated. Lord Shiva had then offered to trap the destructive power of the deluge in his matted hair and only release a part of Ganga's flood upon the earth. This is what had happened.

This story is the most powerful ecological parable we have ever heard. The river, constantly charged by the snow and rain that falls on the Himalayas, could wreak havoc on denuded mountains. But when precipitation is tamed by the forested slopes of Lord Shiva's locks, much of the river's primeval fury is leashed.

But it is still very fierce.

We stood at the edge of a deep gorge cut by the river through the hard, basaltic, rocks of this part of the Himalayas. Here, we met a soft-spoken sadhu carrying a sophisticated camera. He said, "There are many beliefs, many beliefs. On top of Gaumukh…which is 18 km away, at an elevation of 4,255 m…there is a flat piece of land, about 50 sq. miles big. It is guarded by five peaks: the Shivling, Vasuki, Satopanth, Kedarnath and Chaukumbha peaks. That land, it is called the city of Kubera, Alakapuri. Perhaps there are caves beneath." He smiled and nodded to a group of pilgrims. "Then they say that the Ganga actually originates in the sacred Mansarovar Lake through a long, long, tunnel. Which is why it gushes and does not trickle like other ice-melt streams. And here, in Gangotri, this is where Parvati meditated for Shiva. There, you see that stream rushing through the gorge: that is the first tributary of the river. The Kedarganga…though it has some other names as well…comes from Kedarnath. Do you know the difference between the Kedars, the Badris and the Prayags?"

The 18th century temple of Gangotri.

He did not wait for a reply, looking at his watch impatiently. "The Kedars are the thrones of Shiva; the Badris are those of Vishnu; and the Prayags are sacred confluences." He looked at his watch again. "And now I must leave you." He turned away and joined the pilgrims who had wished him. Even renunciants have a hectic schedule.

Enriched by the Kedarganga, the river cascaded over a fall which looked like sculpted coffee-toffee. Here, in the Gaurikund, Parvati used to bathe. "It's very efficacious," said a pretty tourist from Eastern India, "particularly for personal problems."

When we saw the satin smoothness of the rocks, however, we realised that only the most sorely troubled, or the very surefooted, would risk such a stinging sluice-bath.

The very revered Gangotri Temple, standing on its own paved terrace, was a little disappointing: at least from an architectural point of view. We had expected it to have the typical curvilinear spire crowned by a pillared top, unique to many important Himalayan temples. Instead, it had the rather squat appearance we associate with some of the lesser Rajasthani shrines. Rising on a plinth accessed by a few steps, its portico had pillars supporting arches. This was flanked, on both sides, by short towers crowned with domes. Between and behind them was the pyramidal tower that rose above the *garba griha:* the sanctum. Sadly, the sanctum here, like the one in the Yamnotri Temple, did not enshrine the source of the great river. That lay much deeper in the great mountains, as the soft-spoken sadhu with the camera had described.

Later, we learnt that the original temple, built by a Gorkha general named Amar Singh Thapa in the 18th century, had been destroyed by an avalanche. It had then been rebuilt by the princely family of Jaipur. This reconstruction, clearly, accounted for its Rajasthani features.

But then faith is seldom pegged to architectural integrity. Devotees believe that this is the spot where the sacred Ganga came to earth. That faith has given this temple its awesome aura of sanctity as the spiritual source of the holiest river in the world.

Peak
Experiences

KEDARNATH – BADRINATH

If hardship is one of the virtues of a pilgrimage, this journey should have put bright, shimmering, golden, haloes around our heads!

We had driven in from the mountains of Western Garhwal, where the sources of the life-sustaining rivers of Yamuna and Ganga lay, to the less wooded, and more austere ranges of Eastern Garhwal. Very appropriate, of course. Yamuna and Ganga were Mother Goddesses: warm, understanding and nurturing. But Kedar and Badri, as a sadhu in Gangotri had informed us, were the thrones of Lord Shiva and Lord Vishnu, respectively. Fathers, in the traditional mould, are expected to be more strict, more demanding and more distant than mothers.

The crystalline peak of Neelkanth.

The journey was reasonably comfortable and we arrived at the staging post at Gaurikund. No vehicles could go any further.

We looked around, delighted. We were in the midst of the colourful, organised, chaos of a medieval caravanserai. Mules snorted, horses neighed, porters with basket-chair *kandhis* strapped to their backs, importuned, and groups of four, sturdy men, wearing Nepali caps, stood near their *dandi* palanquins eyeing all prospective passengers. One of us had decided to ride, the other had to be consigned to a *dandi* carrying our cameras with an umbrella to protect our equipment from sudden showers. The *dandis* are like long, desiccated, gourds with a chair mounted in the centre and powered by four porters carrying fore and aft cross-poles on their shoulders.

The equestrian partner set off at a fine trot. The palanquin one was raised to shoulder-height and moved, swinging gently, up the crowded pilgrim trail.

Tradition has it that the Goddess Parvati…whose other name is Gauri… meditated in Gaurikund, for years, to become the wife of Lord Shiva. Many young women, yearning to marry the men of their choice, rather than the *suitable boy* selected by their parents, pray here very fervently.

Pilgrims on the Kedarnath trail.

So great is the devotees' trust in the Lord that they believe that if they should die in Kedarnath, or even on the pilgrimage to His temple, their souls will get instant relief from the cycle of births and deaths. They point to Kedarnath's memorial to Adi Sankaracharya as proof of the virtue of surrendering one's life in this hallowed place.

On the pilgrim trail, we trotted and swung past people of all ages, shapes and sizes including whole families and, once, the majority of the residents of a village in the plains of Uttar Pradesh. Most seemed to have no idea of how much they would have to trek or how arduous it would be. Some of the children, and the very old, dozed in *dandis*. Occasionally, small groups who had intended to trudge, stopped horsemen and bargained with them for a ride up the rest of the way.

The terrain became greener, damper, now. Waterfalls tumbled off the cliffs. Sometimes a fine spray slicked the rocks at the side of the road. Wild verbena, with posies of mauve flowers spangled the hillsides. Many of the wayside tea

stalls, thatched with straw and black plastic sheets, had attached dormitories with sacking on the floor and piles of folded woollen blankets.

Seven kilometres from Gaurikund is Rambara. Here, we caught up with each other because the horses had to be watered, fed energy-giving *gur*, and the *dandi*-porters wiped the sweat off their faces, poured water on the ropes holding the cross-poles to the *dandis*, and sat sipping tea. And then we noticed a grey-haired man, with a prosthetic collar, lying in one corner. A blanket covered him, his eyes were closed, and he was gasping. The tea stall owner said that his companions had gone on, hoping that he would recover before they returned from Kedarnath. "Such things are fairly common," the owner said. "In the old days, my grandfather told me, all pilgrims used to perform their last rites before they left home. Nowadays, it is easier. But still the thin air, the cold and the strenuous walk claim their victims every year. Many believe that it is a blessing to die on this pilgrimage."

A road sliced through the cocoa-brown mountains.

We moved on.

Now the terrain changed. Heavily wooded mountains hunched their dark shoulders on the far side of the valley. Bare escarpments rose, curiously moulded like chocolate icing petrified as it flowed, tinsel streams glittering in their rounded shadows. Just before Kedarnath, the mountains became barer, rockier, covered in the moleskin of moss and velvet grass.

Then Kedarnath appeared.

Suddenly there was a great opening in the mountains with the spectacular peaks of its range stretching like a painted backdrop high behind. Two glacial moraines had cascaded down like stony rivers. At the foot of these moraines, and on the far side of the Mandakini River, the temple town spread. It was dominated by the stone tower of its shrine crowned by a metal hat typical of such snow-threatened temples.

We were now standing at an altitude of over 3,500 m. There was appreciably less oxygen here than in the plains but that didn't worry most pilgrims because their lungs had got accustomed to the rarefied air as they trekked up from Son Prayag. If we had had more time on our hands, we'd have opted to stay in the Tourist Bungalow behind the temple. We have been told that the sight of a full moon glittering on the icy peaks rising around Kedarnath is incredibly beautiful.

The temple was reputedly built by the great religious reformer Adi Sankaracharya in the 8th century. It's an impressive stone structure rising on a plinth, with a few steps leading to great door set in heavy stone pillars. This is surmounted by a pediment supporting the sloping roof of the large hall before the sanctum. Above the sanctum rises the stone tower typical of the more important shrines of the Garhwal Himalayas. It is crowned by the hat-like feature that helps ward off damage caused by heavy snowfalls.

Adi Sankaracharya established Kedarnath as one of the four focal points, or *dhams*, of his faith. He died in Kedarnath at the age of 33 and his samadhi lies behind the temple.

We walked past a large cluster of horses and came to an iron bridge spanning the Mandakini. People were bathing in the cold, ice-melt, water. We trod up a steep, cobbled, road leading to the temple. It was lined with shops selling goods used for the rituals of worship and other things in demand by pilgrims: shoes, bags, clothes, hats, trekking sticks, images, votive lamps. On the way up, there was a quaint shrine with a marble statue of Ganga and brass face masks resembling the ones used to embellish the idols of village deities in the Himalayas.

At the entrance to the temple, a monolithic Nandi, the revered bull vehicle of Lord Shiva, gazed at his master enthroned inside. Long queues of devotees had lined up to worship the pinnacle of rock which, in the eyes of their faith, is the Lord of the Mountains, Kedarnath himself. The sacred rock looked like the peak of a mountain, rising from the floor of the shrine.

Above it hung a silver umbrella. For many centuries it had been the focus of the devotion of millions of worshippers and its aura was palpable.

On our way down from the shrine of Kedarnath, the pilgrim who had been gasping in the tea shop was now at peace. His cold face was strangely serene because he was beyond pain and sorrow. The owner of the *chatti*, who had ministered to him during his last hours, said: "He died barely 30 minutes ago. We do not know who he is. His party left him here and went on, saying that rest would cure him. But Lord Kedar thought otherwise. This man was very blessed, very blessed."

On the high road to the Lord, he had taken his last pilgrimage.

Our pilgrimage, however, had not finished. We still had to visit the throne-peak of Lord Vishnu at the 3,133 m high Badrinath.

We had to backtrack a bit, which was comfortable for the one on a horse but rather a jolting, bone-shaking, seat-numbing experience for the one in the *dandi*. The palanquin porters tend to jog downhill and long before we reached the staging post at Gaurikund we would have welcomed a sauna, an oil-massage, a high-protein dinner and a long, long, sleep.

We were still rather groggy the next morning when we left for Gupt Kashi, associated with the legend of Kedarnath. We stopped to photograph the attractive confluence of the Son Ganga and the Mandakini, and then drove up the slope of the Tourist Bungalow in Gupt Kashi. From here we got superb views of interlocking hills, stretching away, terraced and dotted with houses. The Mandakini winds through the bottom of the valley and Chaukhamba rises white and massive at the head. It's not a wide valley but one where the mountains hold their heads far apart and only their feet touch as if they were in slumber. Gupt Kashi, according to legend, is the place where Lord Shiva, in his bovine disguise, went underground to evade the questing Pandavas.

We drove out after lunch and cruised unhurriedly to the beautiful Siyal Saur Tourist Village, situated on the banks of the gushing Mandakini. We checked into one of their log huts. Now, at long last, we really unwound, gave sweets to bright-eyed village children cutting fodder grass, and were lulled to sleep by the sound of the river.

Our night in Siyal Saur worked like a tonic. We woke feeling relaxed and fit and decided to visit the winter home of Lord Kedarnath: Okimath.

It was an interesting old temple in its own walled compound and all the woodwork painted in red, yellow, blue and green. Only the stone tower, and its top hat, were left in their original colours. We noticed a very odd emblem on one side of the tower: a lion holding a tiny elephant in its forepaws. Also, curiously, the main shrine housing the stone lingam with a brass face, was to the side of the entrance hall and not directly in front. Sadly, neither the senior *pujari* nor the younger one could give clear answers to any of our questions.

The beautiful temple of Badrinath welcomes people of all faiths.

Slightly disappointed, we returned to Siyal Saur and reached our room a few seconds before a thunderous storm hit the mountains. Lightning flashed, rain lashed down, and crashing thunder was a brain-numbing cannonade. The power lines shorted and sparked like fire-crackers, and the lights went off.

We woke to a crystal-clear morning scrubbed clean by the storm. At the head of the valley, two snow peaks rose, touched by the sun. The manager of the resort identified them as the 6,931 m high Kedarnath and Sumeru Parbat at 6,331 m. A woman, wrapped in a red dressing gown, stepped out of another log hut, glimpsed the peaks, wrung her hands in excitement and called out to her husband. "Look! Look!" she screamed, "The Crystal Pillars of Heaven!"

We left after breakfast and drove to Rudraprayag. Sunlight streamed down out of a cloudless sky and we had to take off our anoraks and wind down the windows. Standing in a field spangled with drops, a girl in an orange skirt, a scarlet top and blue headscarf, sang as she plucked berries from a raspberry bush. The tune was full of the quavering notes and half-tones that seem to be common to mountain people all over the world.

Kedarnath guarded by the eternal snows.

We stopped at Rudraprayag because it was associated with the great Anglo-Indian hunter-conservationist, Jim Corbett. He had shot a notorious man-eating leopard here and had written a bestseller about it. A little ahead of the spot where there is a road-sign mentioning Corbett's exploits there is also an excellent view of the confluence of the Mandakini and the Alakananda. On an earlier trip we had been able to distinguish the waters of the two rivers very clearly: the blue of the Mandakini and the olive green of the larger river. Now, however, thanks to last night's deluge, they were churning gushes of chocolate brown, heavy with the silt of the mountains.

We had done the drive from Rudraprayag to Joshimath quite often, once with our TV team, so we let this too-familiar road stream by as we skimmed through the notes we had extracted from Gazetteers on Joshimath and Badrinath. Joshimath is both a base for pilgrims journeying to Badrinath and a legend-rich town in its own right. At 1,875 m above sea level, it's scattered over a steep slope above the deep gorge of the Alakananda.

We found the shrines of Joshimath fascinating.

We visited the great old mulberry tree, the largest we have ever seen, under which Adi Sankaracharya is believed to have meditated. Its branches and offshoots have grown together, embracing the old trunk. They look, oddly, like the intertwined bodies of snakes. The tree is often worshipped as the Kalpa Vriksh, The Tree of Wishes; and as an embodiment of the Naga and Nagina serpent deities; as well as for its association with Sankaracharya.

As visitor Jo-Anne Carcle from New York explained to her friends: "You can see what you want in this tree. Nature worship Navajo-style, animism or the purest of philosophies. That's what so great about Hinduism. It's not a dogmatic religion: it's a whole compendium of faiths. You can do your own thing!" Five thousand years of spiritual exploration summed up in a few sentences!

Most of the other important shrines of Joshimath are grouped around an open court and so we were able to visit them in a single morning. Here was the oldest temple, dedicated to Lord Krishna as Vasudeva, facing a shrine to Garuda. An old woman told us that she was the *pujarin*, the priestess, of Garuda. We paid our respects at the shrine of a beautiful dancing Ganesh, another to the benevolent goddess Durga clothed in red, and a third to Navadurga. The Narasingh Temple is particularly important to Joshimath. When Adi Sankaracharya established one of his religious provinces in Joshimath, before fortifying the practice of Hinduism in the temple at Badrinath, he decreed that when winter snows made it impossible for pilgrims to trek to the higher mountains, Lord Badri could be worshiped in the Narasingh Temple. This is still being done.

From sunset to about eight at night, Joshimath is alive with temple bells and bhajans or worshipful songs. But after that, the breeze-whispering stillness of the cool mountains descends on this Himalayan town.

We were refreshed when we joined the second, the 9 a.m., 'gate', to drive up to Badrinath. The road hugs the valley of the Alakananda and its character is dominated by the rushing river and the mountains that hem it in. Thus, because the Alakananda is gentlest at the start of the drive, so is the road. It rises with a certain deceptive docility, a feigned coyness, as it crosses the bridge and winds through rounded, grass-covered, hills. But then, like the river, it begins to assert its true character, forcing its way through deep valleys interlocked like the fingers of hands clasped in prayer. We began to feel the awesome power of the mountains and the river locked in a stubborn, relentless, battle.

We saw the Lakshman Ganga thundering down from the heights of the glacier-fed Lokpal Lake, also known as Hemkund. The terrain grew wilder now, the road steeper and more tortuous. In a stone hut, a water-wheel turned a millstone grinding wheat into flour and covering the miller in fine white dust. Sadhus in saffron declined our offer of a lift, but waved to us with choruses of "Jai Badrinath!"

At Padukeshwar village our convoy stopped, waiting for traffic coming down from Badrinath to build up. Itinerant vendors offered snow-white, hand-spun, hand-woven, woollen shawls as wide and as large as bed-sheets. In the valley below, men and women worked on small, pebbly, fields surrounding a village of slate-roofed huts, stone shrines and two dish antennae gazing up at the sky. Then the policemen blew their whistles. The convoy from Badrinath had come down, we began to move up.

Now, there was a subtle change in the mountains. Slabs of rock rose, glistening as if they had been newly fashioned out of hammered steel. We were approaching the Greater and the Tethys Himalayas. The road became a time-machine spanning millions of years. Conifers thrust out of these shining, stacked, slab-like rocks, their trunks twisted and contorted as if they had been manipulated by a giant bonsai-master.

The air became increasingly chilled and the first glaciers spread stark and white. A gigantic mass of ice and snow overhung a river, another chill blanket of glittering white came down to the road, dripping icy water on our highway. We were now 3,000 m above sea level. A line of perky trekkers marched past, their hiking sticks *clip-clipping!* on the road.

And then, a few hours after we had joined the convoy from Joshimath, Badrinath lay before us. The first sight was a little disappointing. Badrinath seemed to be a random scatter of houses along the lower slopes of a bare mountain. Later, we realised that what we had seen at first were the few buildings on the far side of the Alakananda. The bulk of Badrinath town lies on the nearer side: teeming, congested and polyglot. Pilgrim buses, bulging at the seams, kept disgorging passengers who headed for the *dharamshalas* catering to their particular needs. Restaurants and *dhabas* advertised in Hindi, Marathi, Gujarati, Bengali, Tamil, Telegu and English.

We picked our way through the chaos, to the Tourist Bungalow.

The temple, on the other bank of the river, is a resplendent structure. Its brightly-painted façade, in yellow, red, blue and white, looks like an intricate piece of embroidery rising against scrub-covered slopes. Its large, red and white pennants were starched in the chill wind. It is certainly the most visually-appealing of the Char Dham temples.

After a relaxing sluice-bath in the steaming water from the sulphur springs, we felt more human again. Huddled into our anoraks, we set off to visit the temple.

On the shop-lined road down to the suspension bridge, a burly Sikh visitor explained, very gently, to a couple from Udipi, "Myself and my wife, we regularly take meals from Udipi restaurants in Mumbai. Very healthy, very cheap." A group from Andhra, huddled into overcoats and dressing-gowns, haggled for *Sudarshan Chakras*. The genuine ones have nothing to do with Lord Vishnu's weapon: they're fossilised ammonite mollusks that had lived in the warm Tethys Sea before it was pushed up to become the Himalayas, seventy-five million years ago. We picked our way through the shopping, bargaining, arguing, crowds; strode on to the suspension bridge spanning the turbulent Alakananda; envied the bathers in the "His & Hers" sections of the steaming sulphur springs just above the river; joined the stream of pilgrims trudging up the flight of steps leading to the great, arched, door of the temple.

The entrance to the shrine of Lord Kedar.

As we plodded up, it started to rain: a gentle, penetrating, rain changing occasionally to the soft hail of graupel. Later, when we spoke to the chief priest, as always a Namboodiri from Kerala following a precept laid down by the far-seeing Sankaracharya, he said: "In spite of the cold rain, people stand in a queue, waiting for the blessings of Lord Badri. They are of all religions and, in the Lord, they find the peace they come searching for." Along with us there was a Sikh family, as drenched as we were, and a tall, regal-looking man from Ethiopia wearing an embroidered robe and a knitted cap.

Pressed forward by the crowd of jostling devotees, we were swept through the great doors of the temple into an ante-room and a large hall with chandeliers. Worshippers with offerings stood behind the queue rails waiting their turn to reach the priests standing before the idol of Lord Badri. We tried to get a close look at the idol but were unsuccessful. The shadows, the profuse decorations covering the idol, the jostling crowds, the moving priests, all conspired to give the briefest, most uncertain, glimpses of the dark figure before us. And then, having received our greatly-valued sight of the Lord, our darshan, we were asked to move on and make way for the others waiting impatiently in the queue.

We returned to the Tourist Bungalow when the clouds sat fat and black over Badrinath. A steady drizzle had settled in and the mercury touched nine degrees Celsius, encouraging most people from the warm plains to huddle indoors. A 'local historian', as he called himself, sat with us around a single-bar electric heater which gave a pathetic illusion of warmth. He said, "On cold and gloomy days like this, sometimes the mountains fall, as they have done for centuries, wiping out successive Badrinath Temples." Then, he added, ominously, "Strange creatures are seen prowling around: monster lizards and hairy men, and gold and white snow-lions."

We rewarded him and thanked him for entertaining us. The tales gave a certain piquant, X-Files, quality to the sound of the night wind snuffling in the eaves.

The next morning, the sky cleared and Neelkanth was a glittering diamond between the Nar and Narain Mountains. There is a belief that they are growing closer and closer together and, when they meet, Badrinath will be swallowed up by the earth. But since the Himalayas are growing at the rate of a human fingernail, that cataclysmic event lies, possibly, another millennium away.

From the far side of the valley of the Alakananda came the sound of temple bells and singing. Worship was still alive and thriving at the end of our Yatra.

And that, in our troubled world, was really very reassuring.

The Last Village
in India

MANA

We woke to a beautiful, clear, morning.

Neelkanth stood like a faceted gem clasped in the cleavage of dark mountains: a 6,604 m high peak, glowing at dawn. Yesterday, in Badrinath, it had drizzled for much of the morning and the afternoon, drip-drip-dripping off the eaves, forming bubbles on the puddles, making the mercury plunge to a shivering nine degrees Celsius. Only a maverick

The frontier village of Mana.

The mysterious Saraswati cascades out of the Himalayas beyond Badrinath.

Brahminy Duck, paddling on a reedy pond, seemed happy. The rest of his flock must have winged away to their summer breeding grounds around the glacial lakes of Tibet. And then there were the Alpine Choughs, like perky, yellow-beaked crows, who soared and banked against the leaden sky, and then swooped down to dine on the bread we had thrown out for them.

Since we had come so far, we decided to visit Mana, the last village in India.

As we had expected, Mana was a rugged little settlement. The stone houses, roofed with corrugated iron sheets held down by rocks, or covered with the traditional slate slabs, clustered together for warmth, huddling up the grass-and-boulder strewn slopes. Bundles of faggots had been piled to dry on the roofs and, on top of them, bright woollen clothes had been spread. Beyond and above the village, towered great, bare, mountains rising to snow-dusted peaks. We walked down a narrow, unfenced, path and entered the winding lanes of Mana.

We noticed that the paths between the huts twisted and turned, impeding any draughty winds that might come howling down from the high mountains. But, in spite of the hard lives they must lead, the people were friendly, uncurious. Young girls sat knitting and giggling, older women smiled as they tended to their cattle: short, sturdy, cows, a few goats with long hair, a number of shaggy yak-cow cross-breeds. The traditional dress of the people also showed a distinct cross-border influence: It wasn't quite Tibetan, nor entirely Garhwali. Mana was, in the old Indo-Tibet trading days, at the Indian end of the caravan trail. The people were, clearly, of Indo-Tibetan stock, their lives attuned to the great seasonal cycle of the high Himalayas.

In front of a hut was a little cameo of mountain life. Grandmother Rukhmini sat on a low stone wall cuddling the young Jyotsna. Her other grand-daughter, 12-year-old Deepa, wove a bright chair-rug on the easel of a loom, deftly snipping loose threads with a sharp, curved, knife.

"Deepa has just come from school, and she will go back there. Won't you Deepa?" said her grandmother, hopefully. Deepa smiled and threaded diligently. "Deepa goes to school in Gopeshwar, where we spend the winter. Now the school is closed and she is on holiday. So she is weaving." Deepa began to sing a little song to herself as she worked, clearly enjoying her hobby, not distracted by cell-phones and lap-tops and TV. We'd spotted dish antennas and mobile phone towers in other villages in the mountains so the electronic invasion will not be far behind.

Further up the village, a family sat basking in the sun, a naked infant chortling with delight. "Doesn't the child feel cold?" we asked. Its mother smiled brightly. "This is the height of summer. If we feel cold now, what will happen when the snow falls out of the sky?" We began to feel warm and took off our jackets, even though the temperature could not have been more than 12 C.

The women said, "Few outsiders come here, except the army. You are not army."

We admitted that we weren't. We had come here to see whatever was worth seeing. They had a quick conversation amongst themselves. The baby began to cry. Its mother picked it up and, demurely, put it to her breast covering the infant with her robes. "When a baby drinks, it needs to be kept warm," she explained. Her companions added, "If you follow this track you will come to Bhim's Bridge. Most of those who come here go to Bhim's Bridge."

We trudged along a goat track to the base of a frowning cliff. There, out of the mouth of a cave, gushed a great cascade of water. It foamed down a rocky bed and under an enormous boulder which spanned a steep-sided ravine. We walked across this natural bridge, touched by the cool spray of the waterfall. A *pujari* was sitting near a small stone idol.

"This," he said, "is where Bhim pushed that huge boulder across the river so that the Pandavas could cross it. They were journeying to the higher mountains on their way to the Kingdom Above. And this is the idol of Bhim."

After we made an offering, the pandit rewarded us with an interesting bit of information. "This river," he said, "is the real Saraswati, born inside the mountain. But if you want to know the full story, you must visit the Vyas Gufa, the cave of the sage Vyas. The *pujari* there knows it all."

That, for us, was an irresistible offer.

It was a difficult trek. The track was narrow, bare, boulder-strewn, snaking its way across two rock-and-scree slides, and completely free of the assurance of vegetation. We passed a small, single-celled shrine and asked an old woman, hand-spinning wool into yarn, the name of the idol in the shrine. "It is Ghanta Karan, the guardian of the village. At Dusshera...no it is a festival like Dusshera...he goes down to be with his brother who is in a temple in the main village." She gave us a broad, gap-toothed smile and added, "He and his brother are the guards of Vishnu."

We thanked her and tramped on.

The Cave of Vyas, the Vyas Gufa, is in an interesting rock formation. Its stratification resembles the pages of an ancient book pressed together. Its façade had been whitewashed and, written in red letters on it was the assertion that: This Holy Cave of Shri Vyas is 5,000 Years Old.

Since the Himalayas are millions of years old, this is, in all likelihood, a great understatement.

Inside this unusual cave-shrine the young *pujari* chanted the story of the *gufa*. He punctuated his sentences with loud exclamations of "Hari Om!" which gave his whole narration a rather ritualistic feel as if he were

*The Vyas Gufa where sage Vyas sat to dictate the **Mahabharata** to Lord Ganesh.*

intoning a spell, conjuring ancient spirits to bear witness to his tale. It was rather hypnotic.

"It was here…Hari Om, Hari Om…that sage Vyas sat to dictate the *Mahabharata* to Lord Ganesh…Hari Om, Hari Om. But when the Lord was writing the great epic, his stylus broke…Hari Om, Hari Om…"

We'll edit his narrative but this captures the rhythm of his delivery.

"So what did the Lord do? He broke off one of his own tusks and used it as a quill…So that is why, to this day, Lord Ganesh is known as Ekdanta… and that happened here. In this cave…where we are sitting now…And one thing more…when he was trying to take down what Vyas was saying, the Saraswati…you have seen the Saraswati?…yes, well…the Saraswati was making a great noise…so great that he could not hear the dictation clearly …this made Vyas very angry…he ordered her to divert most of her flow underground…And that is why, today, the Saraswati is, largely, a hidden river. Even so, she is almost as famous as her sisters, Ganga and Yamuna, whom she meets, secretly, in Allahabad…"

He had told his tale very dramatically, almost convincingly. But the fact remained that folklorists had searched for the legendary Saraswati for generations. They had 'discovered' its phantom beds in Haryana and Punjab, Gujarat and Uttar Pradesh but never in the mountains of Garhwal. And yet, since it is linked in legend with the Ganga and the Yamuna, whose sources

The cheerful Indo-Tibetan people of the village.

are in this part of the Himalayas, logic would have placed the source of the Saraswati in this area, too.

We were discussing this between ourselves when we reached the outskirts of Mana. We had stopped beside a rock on which a man was sitting. He was dressed in rough homespun clothes, singing softly to himself. We were taken aback when he spoke to us. "Yes," he said, "we do believe that this rushing stream is the real Saraswati. And that is why we say that we are not the last village in India." He smiled, savouring the moment. "The Aryans came from the north, through many passes in these mountains. One branch of them, holding very important leaders like their general Indra, came through our village Mana. They made their first camp in this land, here: around the river Saraswati. That is why it is so important in the first stories of the Aryans."

He stood up. He was a tall man with grey-blue eyes, brown hair and a slightly freckled face. He looked Indian but he could, as easily, have been a foreigner who had studied our myths and legends. He looked at us solemnly and added, "Which means that Mana is not the last village in India. It is, in truth, the First Village in *Aryavarta: The Land of the Aryans*," and then he loped down into the village and vanished before we could ask his name.

We didn't follow him or try to discover his identity. Sometimes, legends should be left to glow in their own magic.

Matritocracy in the Terai

THE THAARU FEMINISTS

A retired Chief Conservator of Forests told us about them.

He was our neighbour and when he heard we were planning a trip to Dudhwa he said, "Then you must meet the Thaarus." We followed up on his suggestion by reading and talking to other forest officials who had served in the still fairly unknown Terai.

The Terai is a moist seam of forests, marshes and grasslands which stretch at the feet of the Himalayas, watered by the rich, silt-carrying, streams and rivers that flow down from the high mountains. Through it snakes the unfenced boundary between India and Nepal. And across it, unimpeded by frontier formalities, wander a whole, wide-spectrum of wildlife ranging from tigers, leopards and rhinos to the deadliest of them all: the blood-sucking, malaria-carrying, Anopheles mosquito. And also a few hardy forest tribes to whom formal lines drawn on maps have never really mattered.

One such group call themselves the Thaarus. But they were not always forest dwellers. In fact their ancestors lived very far from the lush wetlands of the Terai.

Once upon a time, so their story goes, a group of beautiful Sisodia Rajput princesses were exiled by their father from their kingdom in the deserts of Rajasthan. Though the valiant old warrior was prepared to face a threatened attack, and die honourably in the battlefield, he could not bear the thought of his beautiful daughters committing ritual suicide in the fiery pit of *jauhar*. That was the only

A proud Thaaru woman in her coin-covered blouse.

alternative left for women of noble Rajput blood when faced with the dishonour of capture by their enemies. The proud, white-haired monarch, therefore, summoned some of his bravest old retainers, charged them with the task of guarding their princesses, gave them a posse of tribal Bhil warriors, and sent them to escort his daughters to the safety of a remote Himalayan kingdom with whom he had ties of blood. The feudal families of Nepal and India still intermarry, further strengthening those ancient bonds.

Sadly, during their arduous journey, the old retainers succumbed to malaria and the other debilitating diseases that the Terai produces. Eventually, when the last old Rajputs had died, the princesses realised that they could go no further: neither they nor their posse of Bhils knew the way and delirium had struck the old retainers too swiftly to allow them to speak coherently.

Then, the inevitable happened. The princesses made a pact with their Bhil guards. They would settle down here in a clearing in the Terai, marry their guards, but on one condition. From that day on, their female descendants would always be superior to their males. They would cook food for their husbands and the other males in their family but they would not serve them. To this day, Thaaru women cook their men's food but then they place the *thali* on the floor and kick it towards their men.

That was when we coined the word *Matritocracy: the supremacy of women*. We would have to meet these women who were even more aggressively feminist than the most belligerent of our symbol-burning women's libbers.

On the third day in the dense forests of Dudhwa, we drove into a large clearing. Fields spread, green and burgeoning, groups of tiled huts stood behind high haystacks, and cattle plodded along dusty roads. "This is a Thaaru settlement," our forest guide said.

We tumbled out of our jeep and followed him. As we got closer and closer to the village, men came out to greet us. They were friendly and though they had a trace of the high cheekbones and almond eyes of some of the Himalayan people, and there were also hints of the broad Bhil features, many looked like Rajputs. Or perhaps, we were noticing aspects that we had pre-conditioned our minds to discover! The most striking things about the women, however, were the extraordinarily bright embroidered skirts and backless *cholis* they wore. One, in fact, had a blouse entirely covered in silver coins like an armoured breastplate. They also carried columns of metal bangles on their arms and ankles.

We smiled and started taking pictures of them. At first, the women seemed a little camera-shy but they came out of their shells when we admired their embroidery. And then we got talking to the men. An elder said, "Yes, we are very strict about marriages. If anyone marries outside our four clans, then they will be ostracised. No one will drink water in their house."

Morning in the Terai.

We thought of the rigid, village-imposed, restrictions on such relationships in some rural communities often resulting in the, so-called 'honour killings'.

"Is ostracism the greatest punishment you impose?" we asked.

He looked at us quizzically for a moment and another man in the group said something which even our guide could not understand. Suddenly, everyone began to grin. Our informant shook his head and smiling, asked, "What greater punishment is there than not being able to return home and meet your family and friends? Even death puts an end to all things. But this ...this will be with you as long as you live..." They all nodded their heads, still grinning. Clearly such a dire social penalty had not been imposed for a long time, no one had any anguished memories of such an exile inflicted on anyone they knew or were related to. We admired the social cohesion that seemed to have become such an accepted way of life in this small community.

A hen began to cackle and one of the women, who had been nursing a baby on a rope-strung *khatia* bed outside a hut, got up and lifted the lid off a basket. A hen squawked, flew out, stood in the sun fluffing out her feathers and clucking indignantly. Our guide said, "The fowls are generally bred by the women and girls. They sell the eggs even to their own men. They use their earnings to create their bright garments: it's like...how do you call it? ...a trousseau. The more beautiful the embroidery, the more skilled the girl, the more status she has in this society."

We thought of the old story about the proud princesses and their Bhil guards. We wanted to ask the questions uppermost in our minds but we did not want to do it in front of the women. These women were not the docile, subservient ones we had often encountered in rural northern India: they were proud and independent and more than likely to ridicule our ignorance if we embarrassed them by asking the wrong question. We started strolling out of the village. A few of the men walked with us, the women had stayed behind. We asked the man who had answered most of our questions: "Is it true that the Thaarus are descended from the Sisodia Rajputs?"

He frowned, "So it is said. So it is said." The other men nodded but their faces seemed to be closing up against us. We decided to risk their resentment.

"Do your women have a special way of serving food to their men?"

For a moment their faces got hard and then, probably, they realised that we were trying to be as inoffensive as possible. Some smiled, one laughed. "Some old customs are very difficult to break," he admitted. After a while he asked, "Is it true that some of your families kill girl babies even before they are born?"

That threw us for a moment. Then we said, "Without doubt, some of the old customs are very difficult to break." But, till late that night, in the silence of the dark and primitive Terai, we kept wondering which of the two customs is more civilised: pushing food with your foot in the simple, traditional, Thaaru way, or committing female foeticide in our hi-tech, modern, way.

Between the Road and the River

THE HERITAGE OF MIRZAPUR

It was like a beautiful old book discovered in a dusty antique library.

Mirzapur was rather grimy and neglected: just another fairly large, unkempt, north Indian metro on a bend in the Ganga. Its ghats pierced the cliffs of the river and, from that escarpment, the land sloped down to the town. Our rare *Encyclopaedia Asiatica* said: 'Mirzapur has risen purely for commercial purposes, unconnected with religion or the auspices of royalty. In Mirzapur is seen the best marketplace or *chauk* in the whole of India.'

That was in 1858 when Mirzapur was a trading hub on the Grand Trunk Road built by the Mughals. This great highway had once linked Peshawar in the far north-west of the subcontinent with present-day Kolkata in the east. Mirzapur was about half-way along this arterial route. It was also a riverine port. Here, laden camels and shaggy horses met cargo boats and plodding mule-trains and creaking, covered, bullock-carts which linked India in a network webbing the whole of the land.

This was also the setting, in 1790, when a group of Persian carpet weavers were attacked by dacoits on the highway. According to the legend, still told by the people of Mirzapur, all but one of the travellers were butchered. The master weaver, alone, survived though he was badly wounded and left for dead under a pile of corpses. That was where the people of Ghosia found him. They rescued him, treated his wounds, and nursed him back to health. In gratitude master weaver Sheikh Madarullah settled in Ghosia and began to teach his skills to his newly-found friends. Soon, people

A weaver completes a Mirzapuri carpet, crafted like inlaid jewels.

The idol in Kali-Koh: swallowing all evil.

from the neighbouring village of Madhosingh also became his apprentices and the skills spread across the whole area.

We had first learnt this story on an earlier, and very hurried, visit to Mirzapur. We'd had a phone call from Sheikh Mohammed Razi who claimed to be a direct descendant of the old master weaver. He had confirmed the essence of the story and so we had resolved to re-visit this unassuming town to find out more about these world-renowned, hand-crafted carpets. We did not realise, at that time, that our trip would also lead us much farther afield, deeper and deeper into the distant past.

Beyond the river and the town, the scrub-lands spread with a faint, dry, incense-like aroma. At the end of a rutted, rural, road we stopped at a village of carpet weavers. Most of the carpets are woven in cottages though a few of the weavers had got together and built fairly spacious barn-like buildings for themselves.

The external appearance of the buildings disappointed us, at first. We thought we would encounter a battery of mechanical looms, clacking away, responding to pre-set programmes. We were wrong. When we stepped into the first one, out of the glare of the sunlight outside, our eyes took a while to get accustomed to the comparative gloom. And then, gradually, the colours began to manifest themselves: that's the only way we can describe it. We were in a world of bright, gossamer, webs. They shimmered and stretched row after row, one behind the other. They curtained the weavers but we could discern them moving, crafting swiftly, assiduously, like serried ranks of scurrying spiders. There was a faint, insect-like astringent tang in the air; and a soft *click-snip! click-snip! click-snip!* as if a hundred chitin-covered mandibles were at work.

A slim man with a wispy beard stepped up and gave us a polite *adab* greeting. He said his name was Yusuf. He guided us around, his voice soft and slightly raspy as if the fibres of the wool from Bikaner had lined his throat.

"Yes, Bikaneeri wool is the preferred material," he whispered but, strangely, his voice carried over the *click-snip! click-snip!* of the craftsmen. "Both dyed and undyed wool is used." We had seen small shops in town, packed high with wool of various colours and bundles being carried away in rickshaws, tongas and even on cycles. We stepped out into a yard acrid with the sharp smell of smoke and chemicals. Huge vats bubbled over wood and coal fires. Long spits stood over the vats. They held drums on which wool had been wound in long loops, their ends immersed in the boiling liquid. Bare-bodied, sweat-glistening, men turned the spits, drawing up the steaming, dyed, wool, immersing the rest of the hanks in the hot, liquid, dye.

It seemed to be a very basic, rather primitive, process. But this was just the beginning.

We spent the whole day with the carpet makers and learnt that, over the centuries, they had built on the techniques of the old master weaver from Iran, innovated and even incorporated new materials. They had now evolved two ways of making carpets: tufting and weaving. Tufting is a sort of embroidery. A tough, net-like, backing is stretched tightly over a large screen. The design is drawn on it. The craftsman then uses a device that is a larger version of the implement that peddlers in the streets of many metropolises try to sell to pedestrians to create their own embroidered pictures. The tufter uses this to push coloured threads through the weave of the base net to replicate, in wool, the designs already drawn on the webbing. When the design is complete, it is stuck, using an industrial adhesive, onto a tough fabric. It is then mowed smooth by a machine which looks rather like a large, square iron. Clearly, while tufting is suitable for wall-hangings and room dividers, it is not durable enough for floor coverings.

We walked through the village to a single craftsman's house followed by a Pied Piper tail of children. Looms *clack-clacked* and we breathed the fat, warm, aroma of wool. Woven carpets are created on two types of looms, weaver Abdul Khalik explained in a gracious, old-world, manner. The smaller, strip carpets, are woven on horizontal pit looms by one person; the larger ones are crafted on vertical pit looms by a number of weavers. Mirzapur carpets often capture the more sensitive expressions of Mughal art and resemble the tasteful floral patterns of *pietra dura:* an inlay of semi-precious stones in marble.

But though the Mirzapur weavers are sticklers for quality, they are versatile and not hide-bound by traditional designs. Of late, even East Asian designs have become increasingly popular and the carpet weavers of Mirzapur have used their skills to create Chinese designs with a distinctive Mirzapuri touch.

Towards the end of our tour we visited the showroom of Abdul Jabbar to see some of the great variety of carpets woven by the craftsmen of Mirzapur. And finally, we met the man we'd spoken to on the phone: Sheikh Muhammed Razi. He said, "Yes I am a direct descendant of the original spice and carpet trader who was waylaid by dacoits in this area, but we no longer manufacture carpets, though we deal in them. Buyers from Chile are particularly interested in *durries* with old designs and an antique look." *Durries* are light floor coverings and are 'antiqued' by washing them in caustic soda and sulphuric acid and then rubbing them with a floor polishing stone! Interestingly, Razi also makes carpets from waste leather strips: soft, pliable and durable.

We had steeped ourselves in the lore of Mirzapur carpets. Now we were ready to stride into the centuries before the British and Mughals came to India, far deeper into the past. The next morning we drove to the temples of Vindhyavasini, Kali Koh and Ashtabhuja: all three were crowded with devotees. Worship of the Mother Goddess dates back to, at least, the end of the last Ice Age and many anthropologists believe that the Aryans, with their strongly paternal gods, did not, usually, venture into the harsh, goddess-dominated, lands of the Vindhyas. We did notice that all three goddesses

Rocky paintings in Panchmukh Pahar.

seemed to have been made of black stone and have inserted eyes of silvered metal with black pupils. We have seen such eyes in some Jain statues and were told that the sculpture becomes worthy of reverence only when the eyes have been inserted. The Jains claim that their religion pre-dates Hinduism and this iconographic tradition is, probably, a strong pointer to its great antiquity. To us the idols of the Mother Goddesses radiated a primordial, and rather compelling, power.

We left the ancient temples in quest of more primitive experiences out in the rock-strewn countryside. We scrambled up bare hillocks near Panchmukh Pahar and crawled under overhanging boulders. Here, in their rock shelters, our ancestors had painted their fears and aspirations on the hard walls of their homes. Red ochre figures, out of the Stone Age, danced and hunted animals in what were, probably, magical rites. In those days they needed all the help they could muster: humans were decrepit and awaited death by the age of eighteen. We were gazing through a window into the life and times of a people who had lived here many millennia ago.

Now we left mankind behind and raced back to a time when the earth was very young. The wedge that is now our subcontinent had broken off the great Mother Continent of Gondwanaland and floated, very slowly, on a sea of molten rock called magma, heading for its collision with the continent of Eurasia. On this epic journey, it had crossed a hot spot on the earth near Reunion Island. There, its surface had cracked open and layer after layer of magma had welled through, as lava, and solidified into enormous steps of basalt. Geologists call those steps 'traps' after the Swedish word for stair. We stood looking down at the cascades of Wyndham Falls. The gigantic slabs, over which the Upper Khajori River tumbles, were laid down, by a wounded earth, sixty-five million years ago. We had reached very far back into time, but we still had one more step to take in our quest for the almost-forgotten past.

In a place called Salkhan, we left the car, trudged along a village road, and then climbed up to an outcrop of odd-looking black rocks. On closer inspection they resembled masses of fossilised wood: they had the texture, the grain and the whorls of trees turned into stone. We believed, then, that we were standing in the midst of what must have been a mist-wreathed swamp of giant ferns and horse-tail mosses the size of trees in the Carboniferous Age. All over the world such bog-forests had fallen and created the coal beds and the diamonds of our earth more than three hundred million years ago.

That is what we believed then. Later, we met a Professor, two Doctors and their senior research students in the Geology Department of the University of Lucknow. They did not agree with our presumption that these were petrified wood. According to them, these were fossilised masses of blue-green algae; or the impressions left by them in the sediment at the bottom of the ancient Precambrian Sea. Blue-green algae were the first oxygen-producing creatures

The Wyndham Falls cascading down sixty-five million-year-old trap terraces.

in this world. They were, largely, responsible for converting the poisonous atmosphere of methane, water vapour and ammonia of the early earth into the oxygen-rich one in which we can survive. If our geologists are right, then we have touched a life form that evolved on our earth two thousand five hundred million years ago.

In our quest in Mirzapur we had taken a giant step back in time.

Matters
of Essence

We came to the fragrances via a tiger and a tomb in the Terai.

While shooting a TV travel documentary in the dense forests of Dudhwa we had hit a major obstacle. On principle we had decided to devote just five days on location because that was the time that the average Indian tourist would spend at a destination. And naturally, if we were projecting a National Park known for its tigers, we would have to film a tiger in the wild. But though we had extensive footage on other wildlife, we'd not captured a tiger on our tapes and this was our fourth day.

Just then, a member of our crew, a man who lived near Dudhwa, said, "We should ask Sayeed Baba."

"Who's Sayeed Baba?" we asked.

"He was a fakir who lived in the last century. His ashram was on the river-bank at the edge of the jungle. His touch had the scent of roses and whoever he touched was safe from attack by wild animals. He is also called Sher Baba, the Tiger Baba, by some people."

An interesting story but of no relevance to us. "We've not been attacked by any animals," we said. "Besides, we don't want to be protected from animals, we want to see one: a tiger."

Our informant was persistent. "What harm will there be to go to his tomb? And if you don't want to ask, I will."

So we went to the banks of the Sahali River. Sher Baba's tomb was a simple one: a grave on a platform and covered by a green *chhadar*. Devotees had prayed at the dargah recently and three sticks of incense still smouldered, sending thin, blue-grey, pencils of smoke into the air. They had a dry, resinous, fragrance. Not far from the tomb a number of soiled leaf plates had been tucked under a bush along with a collection of chicken bones and some glittering shards of glass. Strangely, there were no garlands of flowers or petals strewn around. We stood in silence for a moment, filmed the serene scene, and started back to our jeeps.

Just then we, who were the last to leave, stopped abruptly. One of us was, suddenly, enveloped in an overpowering fragrance of roses. And then the fragrance reached the other. It held us for about two minutes and then, slowly, dissipated. But it had been so assertive while it lasted that we spoke about it when we caught up with our TV crew. Our informant, the local man, smiled and said: "The Baba has heard our wish. We shall film our tiger."

We did. On the last day, the last golden rays of sunset spotlighted a magnificent tigress and we captured her on our tapes.

Before we packed up that Dudhwa shoot, the local man said, "Many *mussalmans* like me believe that any *itr* is a sign of blessing, but *itr* of roses is the most powerful blessing of all."

"Are there other attars?" we asked, giving the essence its more usual pronunciation.

"Oh yes, there are many. When you go to Orchha, in Madhya Pradesh, try to meet the itinerant *itr* vendor, Sattar Ali. He knows much about *itrs.*"

By a stroke of luck we were in that beautiful medieval town on the Betwa River on a Sunday: the one day that Sattar Ali comes in from Jhansi, carrying his box of bottles. And he did a good business decanting measured portions of perfumes for visitors to the weekly fair. We, and possibly Pakistan, must be the only countries in the world where the wandering perfumer has survived. This is largely because the distillation of floral essences is still a fairly small-scale industry.

"Where do you get your attars from?" we asked Sattar Ali.

He looked at us through his thick glasses, and probably didn't understand, or didn't choose to understand, our question.

"The best attars come from Kanauj," he said finally. "But the biggest market is in Lucknow. It's been a tradition there from the days of the old Nawabs."

We recalled that rose essence had, traditionally, been a popular perfume in the courts of Islamic rulers worldwide. Its use by the Ottomans of Turkey had led the Europeans to refer to attar as 'Otto of Roses'. Then there was its curious leap across the ocean to America. The Persian term *Gul-ab*, literally Rose Water, had become *Julep* in the Mint-julep, a cool drink favoured by the old plantation owners of the southern states.

We brought our minds back to India.

We were now firmly set on the attar trail, and Lucknow was on our TV itinerary. We visited the perfumery of Mahendra Singh and his son Rajendra. Behind them were glass shelves glittering with crystal bottles holding a great

Left: Sattar Ali, the itinerant perfumer. Facing page: Perfumer Mahendra Singh and his son.

variety of perfumes and their basic essences, the attars.

"Where did your family learn the perfumers' art?" we asked the soft-spoken father and son.

"In Kanauj. Our ancestor was a labourer in a scent-works in Kanauj. No one taught him the secret of extracting these essences. He learnt by looking and working."

"Why Kanauj?"

"It is a tradition there. There are many families with ancestral skills working in Kanauj. Perhaps, at one time, the rulers patronised the profession; perhaps the raw materials...the flowers, the herbs and roots...were easily available there; perhaps it is the quality of the soil and water. In fact, even to this day, the attar called *mitti*...literally 'mud'...is made from balls of the baked earth of Kanauj."

Skilfully, he twisted a gossamer-fine shred of cotton wool onto a sliver of bamboo. Removing the stopper off a glass bottle, he touched the swab to the amber liquid inside, and held it out for us to smell. It had the strong aroma of freshly dug clay: so strong that we recoiled. It conjured up visions of deep earth excavations, dripping tunnels and devastating landslides in our fragile Himalayas.

According to Rajendra Singh, there are five absolute perfumes: rose, jasmine, *mogra*, magnolia and tuber rose. Only absolute perfumes are exported to France.

"Where do you get your flowers from?" we asked.

"From all over. Roses from Aligarh; jasmine from Jaunpur; tuber-roses from West Bengal and Andhra; *mogra* from Kanauj; *keora* from Behrampur," ...there seemed to be no English names for *mogra* and *keora*..."and *henna* from Kanauj and Jaipur."

We drove out to meet another fifth-generation perfumer: Matim Khan.

Lucknow's sun had been beaming bright that day, warming Matim Khan's little office behind his family mansion. An orchestration of attars greeted us: the heat of the day had sent a whole rainbow of perfumes dancing up our noses. The fast-speaking and articulate Matim showed us a printed tariff which listed at least fifteen types of attars including the popular *hina*. This is not *henna* but a blend of flower and spice fragrances, the spice scents being extracted from *jari-booti* which are herbs and roots. The process for all extractions is the same: distillation.

*Chemist Iman Ali adjusts his
attar still.*

An old encyclopaedia in our library says: 'It is generally calculated that 100,000 roses will produce 150 grains of *itr*.'

We then followed one of Matim Khan's employees into an old part of Lucknow, and down narrow lanes where children stopped their play to gape at us. We stepped into a walled yard shaded by a small tree. Here, chemist Iman Ali, with an unlined face and a skull cap, threw wood into an oven. It heated a large-bellied boiler holding rose petals and water. Fragrant steam emerged, condensed, and tricked down a lagged bamboo pipe. It fell, drop by golden drop, into the sandalwood oil at the bottom of the *bhapka* or steam vessel. It was a very basic, a very effective, still. In a room at the far end of the yard, men sat on mats on the floor and stuck labels on vials of the concentrate attar.

Obviously, these attars had to be diluted before they could be sold by vendors, and used as perfumes. But, because of the high concentration of its essence of roses, if a vial of pure attar were poured on the earth as a libation it would seep into the soil and release its compulsive fragrance, slowly, over many days.

And that is what could have happened around the revered tomb of the Tiger Baba in the forested fastnesses of the Terai. Or perhaps we are striving too much to find a rational explanation for a superbly supernal event.

The Aura
of Tehzeeb

LUCKNOW

There is a certain timeless grace about this city.

At the end of a crowded street we drove through the strange Rumi Darwaza. We were told that it was almost three centuries old and resembled a gate in Istanbul. Rum was the old name for Asiatic Turkey, also known as Anatolia. But since we had not heard of major trade links between Lucknow and Turkey, we wondered why a gate had been named after that distant land. "The gate was built by Nawab Asaf ud-Daula in the 18th century" a guide informed us. "He also built the Great Imambara as a famine relief work."

The Great Imambara of Lucknow.

Though the Great Imambara threw no light on the gate, it was an impressive complex with both an inner and an outer gateway set in high walls. On the right, as we entered, was the Asafi Mosque. Ahead, at the end of a pathway stretching through lawns and beds filled with flowers, was the Imambara. The Imambaras, in Shia communities, are, primarily, meant for the laity to hear discourses from their religious leaders the Imams. Here, too, according to the tradition of the Muslims of Lucknow, the colourful replicas of sacred tombs, called *tazias*, are stored for a year before they are taken out in procession during the sacred month of Moharrum, after which they are ritually buried. This custom is unique to the Shias and is not followed by the more traditional Sunnis.

Entombed in the Great Imambara are its creator, Nawab Asaf ud-Daula, his wife Shamsunnisa Begum and the architect, Kifayatullah. And then there is the remarkable architectural maze known as the Bhulbhulaiya. This labyrinth could have been an architectural device to distribute the weight of the upper roof of the main hall and support the weight of the lower one. According to the information board of the Archaeological Survey of India, the pillar-less hall where the religious discourses are given, is 41.71 m by 16.16 m and 14.9 m high: a huge area that called for special engineering techniques.

We had, on an earlier visit, been led into and out of the Bhulbhulaiya. The winding corridors are brightly lit by natural light and well ventilated by windows. Every turn offers four bewildering choices: three are false, one is true. And there is a legend that people who have ventured into this labyrinth without a guide have, often, not been seen again!

A more pleasant tale about the Great Imambara was that the charitable Nawab had had the Great Imambara built as a famine relief work. Rather than humiliate his subjects by offering them a handout, he had asked them to work on building this impressive monument. He had also responded to the sensitivities of the impoverished gentry and nobility. They were given the night shift so that others would not see them at work! He also found fault with the work so that much that what was built by one shift was demolished by the other. This ensured continuing work for everyone as long as the famine lasted.

Finally, this great charitable undertaking resulted in the creation of a very special dish. As the workers had to be given hot food all through the day and night, the Nawab's chefs invented slow, steam, cooking or dum pukht. This evolved into a speciality of Lucknow because even the most delicate flavours are locked in though the ingredients, particularly meat steamed with rice, remain tender.

A picture was beginning to emerge of the relationship between the rulers of this kingdom...known as Avadh or Oudh...and its people. "The first Nawab, Sadat Khan, was a Persian warrior in the Mughal army," our guide

Chikan embroidery could have come from Persia.

said. "He became the governor of Avadh in 1732 and then, as the power of Delhi waned, his descendants became independent rulers. At first their capital was in Faizabad, but the founder's grandson, the charitable Asaf ud-Daula, moved it to Lucknow in 1775, reputedly because he wanted to get away from the dominance of his overbearing mother."

It was probably in the prosperous and secure atmosphere of Lucknow that the nawabs and their subjects cultivated the refined manners and tastes referred to as the *tehzeeb* of Nawabi Lucknow. Most of them were aesthetes who were great patrons of the arts and crafts and loved the good things of life.

The delicate art of chikan embroidery grew under them. "The art could have come from Persia," said chikan dealer Chandraprakash Garg. Women embroidered in the loft of his shop. In his showroom we met young Mohammed Sayed. He collects saris from Chandraprakash every fifteen days, distributes them to women in the villages around, and returns with the finished products. "After labouring in the fields from 6 to 11 in the morning, the women do chikan work in their homes, earning an extra income for themselves," Sayed told us.

It was curious how the heritage of the Nawabs had lived on, and spread, among the common people regardless of caste, creed, or social status. It had an even wider and deeper reach than the rule of the more powerful Mughals and British.

One Nawab, however, became a dedicated Anglophile. In the Little Imambara, where an imprint of the Prophet's foot has been enshrined, we saw a portrait of Nawab Nasir ud-Din Haider. He wore a European-style crown and cloak trimmed with ermine. He also ate like the British and drank with shady European adventurers.

Not that all resident Europeans were charlatans. One of the most remarkable was Claude Martin. He was born in Leon, France, and commissioned as an Ensign in the East India Company in Madras in 1763. We visited the school which, in deference to his wishes, was started in his mansion after his death. La Martinere is in an impressive, rather heavily ostentatious, building. It is permeated with history, nostalgia and, some people believe, a few restless wraiths. Claude Martin was buried in the crypt in his mansion which had once been a strong-room for his friends' valuables.

But for all the good relations that Martin had built up between the Europeans and the people of Lucknow, the overbearing attitude of the British drove a deepening wedge between the races. Eventually, in the middle of the scorching summer of 1857, the long-simmering discontent exploded.

Claude Martin's college, La Martinere.

*When the 140-day siege of The Residency ended on
17 November 1857, five hundred and seventy-seven Europeans
and four hundred and two Indians staggered out to take up the
frayed threads of their lives.*

We visited The Residency, slumbering in the sun, surrounded by the well-tended lawns and gardens maintained by the Archaeological Survey of India. Here a small group of men, women and children had sought refuge from the wrath of a long-abused people. In the basement of one of the old buildings of the Residency there is still a palpable presence of oppressive fatigue, pain and hopelessness. Nevertheless, there were great deeds of heroism and self-sacrifice on both sides.

That evening we experienced a happier aspect of Lucknow and one that is making waves around the world: authentic Avadhi cuisine.

Driving to Nazirabad we walked down a crowded street and entered the MU Eating Point. Here, an array of cooks were flipping romali rotis as light as linen handkerchiefs, grilling skewers of kababs over charcoal fires and frying tikka-like gallawat kababs in a large *tawa*. The owner of the establishment, the tall, heavily-built, Mohammed Usman showed us to a red, laminate-topped, table and brought both gallawat and seekh kababs along with crisp, finger-stinging hot, parathas. He then had a man serve us mutton biryani. The mutton was tender and the biryani had a delicate flavour of saffron. And while we ate under his watchful eye, he spoke about the MU Eating Point and its cuisine.

"My ancestor, Haji Murad Ali, came here about 150 years ago from Bhopal," he explained. "And because he had just one arm, he was referred to as 'Tunda'. At that time, the Nawabs summoned all the great chefs of Avadh and said, 'We haven't the teeth to chew and tear at meat, or the digestions to handle such chunks. Can you create meat dishes to suit our needs?' When the nobles had tried and tasted the dishes of all the chefs, Tunda's name led all the rest."

Clearly his skills had been inherited by his descendants. At this point, however, something nagged in our minds. In their food, dress, customs and faith, the Nawabs of Avadh followed traditions that were alien to the Hindus over whom they ruled. Or were they?

Some years ago we bought a book titled *Lucknow: the Last Phase of an Oriental Culture* by Abdul Halim Sharar. We had carried it with us. There is an interesting comment in it which says: 'Islam…underwent significant changes through Sufi beliefs which were influenced by Hindu Vedanta and yogic philosophies.'

The Residency, surrounded by well-tended gardens.

We recall that Sufism is a spiritual path which recognises the intrinsic oneness of all creation and uses religious ecstasy to experience a personal contact with the Creator. It is much like the Bhakti Movement in Hinduism and the Charismatic Movement in Christianity. Many of the Nawabs, we understand, were Sufis. Rulers who accept such a belief would tend to be tolerant, benign and gracious. Rather than erect barriers between seemingly divergent faiths and communities, they would strive to build bridges emphasising convergences, highlighting similarities. The fountainhead of Sufism is Konya in Turkey where the great mystic Maulana Jalal ud-din Rumi lived and died. Lucknow's Rumi Darwaza is, thus, more than a gate to the route to Turkey.

It could, we believe, explain the *Lucknawi's* sustained and graceful urbanity, their *tehzeeb,* moulded by gentle encounters through their own Rumi *darwazas.*

Pastures of the
Blue Lord

THE BRAJ

Now we have entered a whole region soaked in legend and reverence.

We drove in from Delhi, through fields of yellow mustard, to mythic Mathura. When we boarded a skiff and were rowed out on to the slow-flowing Jamuna, the steps and arches and ribbed cupolas of the Vishram Ghat became an antique woodcut gazing down at its own reflection. Beyond the town spread the lands now known as the Braj. And this is where our voyage into the landscape of legends began.

We have with us Abraham Eraly's superbly researched and evocatively written book, *Gem in the Lotus, the Seeding of Indian Civilisation*. According to Eraly, the Aryans had moved out of their first home in India, the Punjab, and into this Gangetic Plain: 'Though agriculture now steadily gained in prominence, society still remained substantially pastoral during the entire Vedic period...In rural India, wealth continued to be measured in cattle.'

In a pavilion at the Kusum Sagar, a loving cameo of affection.

A pastoral people spoke a pastoral language and gave cattle-based words extended meanings. The Vedic word for war was *gavisti,* meaning 'desire for cows'. War was, primarily, a cattle raid for early Aryans. Dusk was *go-dhuli:* literally 'cow-dust' time when herdsmen and their cattle, plodding home after a day of grazing in the pasture-lands, raise clouds of dust in the saffron sunset. The *Braj Bhoomi* was, the 'Land of the encampment of herdsmen'. A *gotra,* which was a cow-pen, also became a lineage group, a clan.

The most powerful of the pastoral clans, was the Yadavas. As the encampments of herdsmen grew into villages, the villages into hamlets, towns and cities, so did the might of the Yadavas. One of them, Kamsa, became the king of the territory whose capital was this prosperous riverine metropolis: Mathura. Significantly, though Mathura had grown into a great capital, its name still captured its pastoral origins. Mathura is, literally, The Town of Churns. But, as often happens to rulers ensconced in powerful capitals, Kamsa fell prey to mounting fears based on a prophecy. He began to believe that he would be killed by his own nephew, one of the sons of his cousin, Devaki and her husband Vasudev. He threw his sister into prison. Here, Devaki gave birth to six sons, in succession. And when each one was born, the infant was slaughtered on the orders of the despot.

The parallels between this story and the Christian one of the Massacre of the Innocents by Herod, are striking.

The embryo of the seventh son was miraculously transferred into the womb of Rohini, another of Vasudev's wives.

On the birth of the eighth son, Krishna, the Swarthy One, another miracle happened and Vasudev was able to spirit him away and place him in the care of Yashoda and her husband Nanda, chieftain of the cowherds' village of Nandgaon. The infant's brother, Balarama, had stayed with his mother Rohini in Gokul, across the river from Nandgaon. These two children, of royal blood, became cowherds, grazing their cattle in the pastures of the Braj. But though they had had the same upbringing, their characters were markedly different.

Balarama was noted for his strength, fearlessness and skill with his plough: he was more a farmer than a herdsman. Krishna was handsome, charming and an accomplished flautist and he fitted easily into the pastoral way of life. Their friends were the young herdspeople of the Braj. Krishna's closest, and most loving, companion was the beautiful milkmaid Radha of the village of Barsana.

Our quest in the Braj began with a visit to the birthplace of the Blue Lord, in Mathura.

An old shrine marks the prison cell where the Lord was born. We walked down a corridor and entered the small prison room. A low platform indicated the place where Devaki is believed to have given birth to Krishna. On the walls

Like an old woodcut: Mathura's Vishram Ghat.

were depictions of Brahma, the Creator, Vishnu, the Preserver, and Shiva, the Destroyer. There was also a portrayal of the Infant Krishna being carried across the Jamuna, shielded by the multiple hoods of the immortal serpent, Sheshnag. In a tangential belief, Balarama is said to be an incarnation of this great snake which gives an insight into the complexity of *Krishnalila: The Charisma of Krishna.*

Leading on from this cell is the resplendent Shri Krishna Janmabhoomi Temple, with marble idols of Radha and Krishna and an unusual column which the priests insisted was made of mercury. Since that metal is normally liquid at room temperature if, indeed, this silvery-grey *linga* is made of quicksilver then ancient Indian savants must have used a very special technique to solidify it.

We left the apparent metallurgical mystery of Mathura and drove further into the Braj.

Our prime purpose in coming here was to witness a most unusual Holi festival which, though based on the gentle pastoral life, has taken on far more vigorous overtones. On the way, however, we had decided to visit some of the places associated with the greatly-loved herdsman Prince, now recognised as the eighth incarnation of the Preserver.

As we drove on, we noticed that most of the pasture lands have been converted into green fields and thriving farms. Though there were a few hillocks and ravines rough with scrub, there were also a number of water-bodies. Such water-conservation systems of ancient India still recharge the aquifers, ensuring that village wells seldom go dry.

We stopped at the Kusum Sagar. There were three beautiful pavilions built on the far bank and accessed by a parapet that ran alongside the ghats. According to the old watchman, the elegant *chhatris* were "Very old" and so were the murals painted inside them. One, in particular, caught our eyes. It showed Radha reclining on a chair and looking at herself in a hand-held mirror. Seated behind her, and attending to her hair, was Krishna, identified by his iconic peacock plume. It was one of the most tender and loving cameos of affection that we have ever seen.

We drove on, past increasing numbers of pilgrims and piles of brushwood at the crossroads where the cleansing Holi fires would be lit.

We drew up again at another ancient reservoir: the enormous Mansi Ganga. Boatmen plied across it, disturbing the reflections of the temples and old mansions built on its banks. Pilgrims hurried down the narrow lanes of the market, determined to complete their long circumambulation of the major shrines of the Braj. This includes the 22 km road around the sandstone ridge known as Govardhan.

After their arduous pilgrimage, devotees bathe in the Mansi Ganga and carry some of its water into the Giri Ram Govardhan Dan Temple. This unusual place of worship has a covered court which can be seen from the

Guarded entrance to the legendary birthplace of Lord Krishna.

road. In the centre of this court is a tree. At the base of this tree is a small shrine built around a black rock. The rock, reputedly, is the peak of the Govardhan hillock and is the idol around which the temple has been built. Pilgrims who have completed the circumambulation then pour libations of Mansi Ganga water on it.

People in temple towns, we have found, are often eager to inform visitors about the special features of their shrines. A man in his twenties, wearing a spotlessly white kurta-pajama, walked up to us as we were looking down at the temple. He wished us politely and asked,

"Do you know what that rock is? What the idol is?"

"We've been told it's the peak of Govardhan Hill."

"Yes," he said, doubtfully. "Perhaps. But Govardhan Hill is of sand colour. This rock is black."

We nodded.

"The rock is the finger of Lord Gopinath. That is why it is black."

Gopinath, Lord of the Milkmaids, is another name for Krishna. "Are you going to see the Lat Mar Holi of Barsana?" he asked.

We said we were.

"Then you should hurry. The crowds have already gathered. And I can hear the drums beating."

We had to drive slowly through the festive crowds, past the Pan Sarovar Tank which The Blue Lord had sanctified because he used to bathe his cattle in it, and also as the scene of his occasional trysts with Radha.

Over the generations, the poets of the Braj had woven the tales of Radha and Krishna into Holi. According to the bards, Lord Krishna was so fond of eating cream, yoghurt and butter that, when the milkmaids of Radha's Barsana refused to give him any, he broke their pots. This led to a fight between the people of Barsana and those of the Lord's Nandgaon: a conflict that is re-enacted here every year.

We drove down a rural road, through the fields and scrub of the Braj, and looked across a stretch of water. Crowning the peak of a hill on the far side, rose the white temple of Nandgaon. People, ant-small in the distance,

Devotees believe that Lord Krishna raised this hillock aloft, on his little finger, and held it up for a week to shield his people from a deluge. Two of the pilgrims, a man and a woman, were inch-worming their way down the road. They prostrated themselves with their arms extended above their heads and carrying a pebble to mark the end of their reach. They then rose, stepped up to the stone, prostrated themselves again. They would use the length of their bodies to measure the entire 22 km of the sacred **parikarama** *encircling Govardhan.*

The festive mayhem at Lat Mar Holi.

climbed to the top and made their way down again. It is customary to seek
the blessings of one's favourite deity before indulging in the violence of the
Lat Mar Holi: literally The Holi of the Belabouring Staves.

We entered Barsana and parked our car in the playing fields of an old
village school, and then joined the jostling crowds streaming into the narrow
lanes where the encounter would be staged. People were jammed into the
balconies and terraces on both sides of the road. Bursts of coloured powder
exploded over us but there was no sense of menace in spite of being part of
a teeming, moving, mass of people. We shuffled our way into the narrow
Rangali Gali, the Colourful Alley and scrambled on to a perch on a platform
just off the lane. The crowd continued to swell till every inch of the road and
the balconied houses rising on both sides was massed with spectators.

Then, down a feeder lane, yellow robed and turbaned Goswami priests
began to chant. Sitting next to us was a brisk district official, formal in a
black Nehru jacket. He turned to us and explained, "The ancestors of the
Goswamis had come from Bengal early in the 16th century." We thanked
him and picked our way across to the Goswamis, clouds of coloured powder
continuing to shower down on us from the balconies above.

We asked one of the old priests, "What is the significance of Lat Mar Holi?"
He frowned for a moment, then smiled like a child. "In Braj everything is the
play of the Lord. It is all his *lila*. You must not question. You must experience."
We absorbed this Zen aphorism and returned to our perch.

The entrance to Baldeo's town, Gokul.

Great drums began to boom even before the Goswamis' chants had ended. The drums were mounted on wheels, trundled and struck by sweating, colour-smeared, men wielding drum-sticks with great gusto while others walked behind them singing with more enthusiasm than skill. They were the heralds announcing the opening of the whacking tournament.

Then the gladiators arrived. The courageous men of Nandgaon, successors to the milkmaid-teasing companions of Krishna, were dressed in yellow, wore padded turbans secured around their chins, and carried padded leather shields. Miraculously, the crowds filling Rangali Gali moved back, making room for the Nandgaon volunteers. Colours continued to rain down on us.

There was an audible intake of breaths from the crowd and all heads turned to the entrance to the road. The aggressive women of Barsana had appeared, bustling down the Rangali Gali. They wore pink or yellow saris and every one of them was armed with a sturdy staff about two metres long. They formed up on both sides of the crowded alley with the Nandgaon men sandwiched between them.

We felt the tension in the crowd building up.

Suddenly, without any perceptible signal, the beating began. We heard the sound of the blows before we realised what was happening.

Nandgaon men were crouched on the road, their shields protecting their heads, while vengeful Barsana women raised their staves and belaboured the men's shields with all the force they could muster. They lifted their *lathis*, leapt, and whacked the leather shields with frenzied *smack-thud! smack-thud! smack-thud!* viciousness.

We were amazed, than appalled, then alarmed. This was no ceremony, no stylised ritual. This was a catharsis. Pent up anger and frustration unleashed against oppressors. A once-a-year explosion of socially sanctioned violence: the, so-called, Battle of the Sexes personified in an explosion of rage that must have reached deep into the psyches of every man and woman present.

It went on for four hours: women smiting men, men crouching in submission, coloured dust enveloping us like powdered blood, a cacophony of voices merging with the unrelenting *thud! thud! smack! smack!* It was uncontrolled mayhem.

Or was it mayhem? In all this apparent violence, not a single man from Nandgaon got hurt.

But we, certainly, were emotionally drained; the coloured powders of Holi caked on our sweat-wet bodies.

Eventually, a priest stepped in and raised his hands. The violence ceased. The crouching men staggered to their feet. The women rested on their staves, breathing hard. Slowly, the crowd began to disperse, mingling with the belaboured men of Nandgaon and the exhausted women of Barsana, streaming away down the brilliantly coloured Rangali Gali.

The drums of Holi throbbed like the reassuring heartbeat of the Braj all through the night.

The next morning, still feeling a little drained, we drove across to Baldeo, a temple dedicated to Balarama. On the narrow road leading to the temple were shops glittering with pyramids of *misri*, crystalline sugar-candy, the approved offering to Balarama. We stepped in through a gateway and down into an open court encircled by a gallery. In the centre of the court was a small temple with a shrine to the elder brother of Lord Krishna. In the court, a line of women in colourful saris sat in front of a group of singers and musicians: a blind drummer, a harmonium player and others who kept time by striking together two strips of wood on which small cymbals had been mounted. The song and the music had a very infectious beat which got the women clapping in unison.

After a while, a woman in a blue sari got up and began to dance with sinuous grace and considerable sensuousness, moving her hands, hips and body and, often, swirling around. Soon she was joined by others and they became a gyrating blur of colour. It was a fascinating, stimulating, spontaneous performance. Then the musicians took a long break and we found that the sanctum door of the temple had been opened and the *pujaris* were attending to the idol.

We stepped forward and looked in. It was a black idol with large, round, staring white eyes with black pupils. But why was it a black idol when, according to the prevailing belief, Balarama was fair?

Then we recalled what the old Goswami priest had said about the Blue Lord of the Braj. "It is all his *lila*. You must not question. You must experience." Or, as our prayers say in acceptance of the Divine Will: Amen.

Domain of the Holy Exiles

CHITRAKOOT

Chitrakoot is a Power Spot.

There is a gritty vitality about this riverine frontier town split between Uttar Pradesh and Madhya Pradesh. Chitrakoot stands in rugged ravine country where men wear fearsome moustaches and sling shotguns even when they perch precariously on the roofs of crowded buses.

"But never fear for such men-folk" our guide assured us. "Even the most terrible *dakus* would never harm anyone in Chitrakoot. The presence of Lord Rama, Lakshmana and Sita is too powerful here. You are knowing the story?" he asked.

The ghats at Chitrakoot.

We said we did.

The *Ramayana* is one of the greatest, and longest, epics in the world. It tells the story of Rama, a prince of the prosperous kingdom of Ayodhya, being deprived of his birthright for fourteen years by a scheming stepmother. He, his brother Lakshmana and his wife Sita are forced to wander in the wilderness of our central Indian badlands as exiles, exposed to many hardships and adventures till, at long last, they return to claim what is rightfully theirs. Their encounters become parables to highlight the virtues of heroism and nobility and the triumph of righteousness. Using the *Ramayana* as a guide we had decided to rediscover the epic foundations of Chitrakoot. According to our copy of the *Ramayana* by the famed scholar C. Rajagopalachari, commenting on the royal exiles' sojourn in this revered town, their "happy life in Chitrakoota is a wonderful background to set off the later sufferings and sorrows of the three".

"So then you are also knowing the dharma of this holy place," smiled the guide. "So please walk on the ghats and enjoy!" He waved his hand cheerily and ambled away.

The serene ghats were gilded by sunset, with the flowing Mandakini River *lap-lap-lapping* on the water-varnished steps. We strolled around in the soft light of dusk and then returned the next morning, a little after dawn had silvered the Mandakini. The ghats were alive.

Long flights of landing steps, crowded with people, led up from the lapping river. Ferrymen waited expectantly, their canopied barges shimmer-rustling with tinsel streamers. Devotees stood waist-deep in the flowing river, worshipping the dawn with an oblation. Viewing the rising sun from across a sheet of water is believed to strengthen the eyes. This is also the time when there is a tintinnabulation of bells ringing in the shrines, the haunting calls of conches, the chants of voices raised in prayer. Blue incense wafted down from the temples and its resinous fragrance mingled with the broad, ozone, scent of the river. People washed their clothes, dried them like fluttering banners, backlit and translucent in the rising sun. Men sluiced down the ghats with metal buckets filled with river water and, on a platform in front of a shrine, an elephant caressed the head of a young priest while a daubed mendicant looked on, coldly aloof.

Ram Ghat is the focal point of Chitrakoot. Here, writes Rajagopalachari, Rama said to Sita, "This hill is our Ayodhya. The birds and beasts are our subjects. The Mandakini is our Sarayu." As in all pilgrim spots, legend

Above: After this the beloved Godavari vanishes underground.
Facing page: A decorated boat in Chitrakoot.

and embellishment grow around the original saga. We had now begun to experience the *Ramayana* as it had been richly embroidered in Chitrakoot. Here, too, is the Tulsi Chabutra, the platform on the Ram Ghat where the great poet-saint Tulsidas is said to have written his version of the *Ramayana*.

Rising above Ram Ghat were such reputedly ancient temples as the Param Kutir, and the Yagya Vedi going back to the very origins of the universe, according to the resident priest.

The name 'Param Kutir' echoes the common ancestor of Hindi and English. It means the 'Prime Cottage' in which the three royal exiles lived.

Our *Ramayana* says: 'Lakshmana was a clever workman. He soon constructed a strong hut, which was weather-proof and made it comfortable and convenient. Single-handed, he completed the mud hut with windows and doors all made of bamboo and jungle material.'

Clearly, such a fragile hut could not last the eons which have lapsed since the age of Lord Rama. The Param Kutir has been reconstructed as a modern, though tastefully simple, temple, popular with worshippers today. We walked up to it, queued up behind a group of devotees, and heard a little boy with an elfin face and a bright expression ask his father, "But if all this was a jungle when Lord Rama, Sita and Lakshmana were here why are they wearing such fancy clothes? Dadima said that they dressed in animal skins and leaves and bark?" His father laughed nervously and looked around at the other devotees, and then said, "This is how the *pujaris* have dressed them," and then raised his finger to his lips cautioning his son to a discreet silence.

Lord Rama's younger brother, Bharata, came to Chitrakoot to persuade the Prince to return from exile and assume his rightful position as ruler of Ayodhya. Rama, however, refused to return till his term of banishment had been completed but, according to a local legend, Bharata and his army of 'chariots, elephants, horses and foot soldiers', as well as the royal family and nobility of Ayodhya, had camped for a long while a little below Param Kutir. Today, that spot is marked by the Bharat Mandir where the whole court is displayed in a diorama of little idols, worshipped by devotees and admired and photographed by tourists for their doll-like authenticity.

But there is a slight difference of opinion here. Some devotees believe that the great Darbar of Bharat was held in the Yagya Vedi, or the Brahma Temple, adjoining the Param Kutir. When we trudged up to it, we learnt that this temple has a much older association. A local priest told us that, before creating the universe, Lord Brahma had performed a powerful ritual with 108 fires here. Only one of these fire pits remains, however, and though it looks like a fairly modern shallow well, pilgrims still revere it with their offerings.

The fires of creation, in a way, did fashion the landscape of Chitrakoot. According to geologists, the step-like structures of the Deccan Trap were formed by lava welling up from the depths of the earth. Consequently, around Chitrakoot, there are huge caves and other sites associated with that great exile.

Above: The ghats.
Facing page: A devotee reads the epic **Ramayana**.

The temple in Hanuman Dhara.

Out of Chitrakoot we drove, 18 km along a rural road, bringing us closer and closer to a range of mountains. They are largely scrub covered now, dotted with the green puffs of bamboo thickets, but at the time of the exile they were covered with dense forests, according to the saga. We left our car at the base of an escarpment and climbed a flight of steps bordered by a stream gushing out of a cave. A group of people chanted, clapping their hands and swaying in veneration. We climbed to a higher cave with a narrow entrance like the proverbial eye of a needle. Inside, the cavern widened and little bats hung in clusters, like grapes, from the ceiling, their sharp, cloying, odour oppressive in the still, damp air. Some of the other visitors began to pant, claiming that they felt suffocated. Ahead of us the cave opened to a much larger chamber and the claustrophobia eased.

We walked ahead and joined a group of devotees standing around a pool in which water bubbled from an underground spring. This cave is called Gupt Godavari where, according to a local belief, Sita had bathed and almost fallen a victim to an evil *asura*. But the fearsome creature had been turned into stone by the vigilant Lakshmana, and it still hangs, like an ugly mass of rock, from the ceiling of the cave.

The water from this revered spring appears again as a stream in the lower cave, and then cascades down the hill to disappear underground again and reappear, according to our guide, on Mount Brahmagiri, near Maharashtra's Trimbakeshwar. "It is a very wonderful thing, no?"

We agreed that it was, indeed, amazing. Does the river really flow, hidden, halfway across India? Does the belief here, in this cave, enshrine a subterranean truth unknown to geographers?

Driving back into Chitrakoot and out, we followed the course of the Mandakini to a place called Sati Anasuya. Here, a fairly large temple-complex rises above the road which runs along the bank of a wooded stream. The temple, we were told, marks the site of the forest hermitage, the ashram, of the legendary sage Atri Muni and his virtuous and beautiful wife, Anasuya.

Inside the temple there were unusual idols: a cradle with three babies. A priest told us the strange story of this triple idol with many pauses for effect, repetitions, and exclamations at the truly wondrous parts.

"In legendary times, perhaps ten lakh years ago, perhaps more, who knows, Atri Muni had his hermitage here. He had a very beautiful wife but… *wah! wah!*…she was also very virtuous. So she could be left alone while he meditated on that rock, sticking out from the cliff, far above. You see those hives of rock bees, very dangerous, but they never touched the sage, such was his power…*wah! wah!*"

We decided to paraphrase his tale, dropping his exclamations.

One day, when Atri was on his high, rocky perch, the Trinity of gods, Brahma, the Creator, Vishnu, the Preserver, and Shiva, the Destroyer, decided to test the virtue of Anasuya. They disguised themselves as mendicants, came to the hermitage, and demanded food. But they also said that they had taken a vow that they would accept a meal only from a naked woman. If she had acceded to their wishes, she'd have lost her virtue; but if she refused to give them food according to their vow, she'd have sinned grievously. The merits of her unsullied virtue, however, came to her aid. In the blink of an eye, the three divine mendicants were turned into babies. Relieved, Anasuya picked them up and nursed them at her naked breasts!

Out of Sati Anasuya we drove, heading for the monkey-haunted heights of Hanuman Dhara. Eagles soared above us as we climbed a winding path up the hill, past tribes of grey-furred *langur* monkeys, into the cliff-side shrine of Hanuman. That great general had attacked the palace of King Ravana in Sri Lanka because Ravana had abducted Sita. Hanuman had then come here to cool himself after a fiery battle. His red idol is still cooled by a spring of water gushing out of the hills of Hanuman Dhara. This local legend is at variance with the *Ramayana* but, clearly, the long line of devotees who climbed the hill believe it implicitly.

Stepping out of his shrine we stood on the edge of the cliff and looked across at the ravine-riven lands of this holy town. Why had Lord Rama, later revered as the seventh incarnation of the Preserver, Vishnu, chosen this place for his exile? Was he searching for something, some way to reconcile his duty with the hardships that had been inflicted on him so unfairly? What

The Mandakini at Sati Anasuya.

could he have hoped to find in this remote wilderness? There had to be an explanation somewhere in Chitrakoot.

At the base of the bow-shaped Kamadgiri Hill, sometimes called The Chitrakoot Hill, a teacher in a white robe sat on a platform under a tree, speaking softly. Below the platform, a number of people sat, or stood, listening to him with rapt attention. About a third of them were foreigners, both Caucasians and Asians. We joined the group and the teacher nodded to us, smiled slightly, and continued with his talk. He spoke in very simple Hindi, translating terms, occasionally, into English. Much of it was a commentary on the great exile but one unusual part caught our imaginations. He said:

"And so, as I have told you, Chitrakoot has a much deeper significance than the eye can see or the other senses can tell you. Can you sense the substance that carries light? But it is real. Can you sense radio or TV waves? But they, too, are real. So there is a belief, a very strong belief, here, that this mountain behind us, Kamadgiri, is very special. Pilgrims walk barefoot around this mountain, convinced that this spot, hallowed by the royal exiles and the sages, would grant their wishes. Why so? Because this mountain is special. It is believed by many that Kamadgiri is hollow."

He paused, nodded to himself as if to emphasise what he had said, before continuing:

"The hollow mountain is said to have four doors: the Pramukh Dwar, or main entrance, which is now a shrine, and three other portals. No ordinary human has crossed this mysterious threshold and seen the great lake inside Kamadgiri, but there's a curious phenomena associated with this mountain. Rain falling on the protected trees of this hill does not run off. It sinks in and then emerges as 360 springs, which start flowing at the same time as if they were the outlets of an overflowing underground lake."

He paused again, looked around and asked, "Any questions?"

A man with high cheekbones and shoulder-length brown hair, wearing a brown khadi kurta and jeans asked, "What is so special about underground lake, Guruji. There are many such around the world." He had a marked Russian accent and he carried a cloth bag *Going...Going...GOA.*

The teacher looked at him and said, in English, "That is a good question. Thank you." And then he reverted to his simple Hindi. "Around this lake, it is believed, sages sit in deep meditation. They are bathed in a blue light which keeps them immortal. They are the Masters of the World given the responsibility to make certain that we do not destroy ourselves. And through their thoughts, they influence the minds of leaders and even physical events."

Some of the foreigners stirred restlessly. One of them expressed a doubt that had risen in our minds. A woman, British by her accent, with a shaven head and a white sari, said, "Sir, that sounds like science fiction."

The darbar.

Many of the other listeners turned, glaring at her. But the teacher was unperturbed. He replied in English, "Yes Marion, it does. But then. The submarine was conceived by writer Jules Verne, and it became reality. So did landing on the moon." He stood up very gracefully, did a deep namaste to all of us, leapt lightly down from the platform, and walked away.

We drove back to Ram Ghat just as dusk was settling on the river. Bells rang and incense draped its veils of perfume around us as the beautiful evening ceremony of *aarti* filled the temples with the soft light of oil lamps and chanting. A timeless heritage was being evoked again with particular nostalgia as day gave way to night and the stars began to appear, tentatively, in the sky.

Groups of women sat in a circle, holding tiny candles, doing their own, very simple, but deeply moving *aarti*. Or perhaps it was some other traditional ceremony of remembrance which their mothers had done before them and their grandmothers even earlier, and on and on and on back through the mists of time when, out of the forests emerged a Prince, his Wife and his devoted Brother and stood on the banks of the Mandakini River.

That night, back in our room, we got out our copy of the *Ramayana*. There, very clearly, it was said that the royal exiles had been advised to come to Chitrakoot Hill by Rishi Bharadwaj. Had they been sent here because of the powerful influence that would be exercised over them by the seers hidden in the hollow mountain?

It sounded like fantasy then, but now, that we come to think of it, so did Communication Satellites when first conceived of by science-fiction writer Arthur C. Clarke.

The Garden of Fidai Khan

PINJORE

The Mughals knew how to relax.

The Mongols from the steppes had been go-getters, and very ferocious ones at that. But when they had settled in India, and become Mughals, they had changed. They had constructed highways and planted avenues of trees to give shade and fruit to travellers. They had dug wells and built serais to shelter the weary wayfarer. They had erected *kos minars* as distance markers and staging posts.

And they had created the most beautiful gardens.

After a long and rather taxing trip abroad, we drove through the golden, mustard, fields of Haryana, and into the Mughal Gardens of Pinjore. They are the only Mughal gardens in which one can spend a night, thanks to the innovative ideas of their designer, the famed 17th century architect, Nawab Fidai Khan. Today he would have been acclaimed as a man who thought out-of-the-box, which is probably why he was made the Governor of the Punjab by the Mughal Emperor Aurangzeb. Fidai Khan's creativity is what gives the Yadavindra Gardens at Pinjore their special character. And also the two levels at which they can be enjoyed.

Primarily, they were created for relaxation, and this is what drew us, and most of the other visitors, to Pinjore.

Every morning, but more so on holidays, crowds of visitors enter the gardens and spend an unwinding day strolling and relaxing on the lawns, or dining in the Golden Oriel Restaurant. We joined them and found that most

The elegant serenity of Pinjore at dusk.

were in family groups with a fair sprinkling of self-conscious honeymooners and a number of high-school and college-going kids. But even on holidays or long weekends, only the lawns around the water course and fountains are crowded. The rest of the grounds are so extensive, the winding paths through the orchards have been so carefully planned, that those who want to be left alone can easily get away. This time we had decided to spend two nights in the Sheesh Mahal, above the entrance to the gardens. It had a ceiling with mirror inserts, accounting for its name 'The Mirror Palace', a view all down the long fountain-tinkling water course extending to the pavilion-apartments at the far end, and a marble paving stone which we could remove if we wanted to cool our feet in flowing water!

The 'Painted Palace', the Rang Mahal, at the other end of the water course, was a little more ornate because it had been the suite of the Maharajas of Patiala. It also had a regal Penthouse Apartment.

That night, Pinjore took on a new dimension. After the day-trippers had left at 10, the fountains switched off, the lights in the gardens dimmed, Pinjore belonged to us. The long water courses rippled gently, lit only by the distant stars. The pavilions seemed unreal: settings in some long-forgotten fairy tale. A breeze whispered through the dark trees, a night bird called. It was very still, very serene, very restful.

We woke early, that first morning, and walked alone in the quiet, pre-dawn light. There was the gossamer tang of woods-smoke and we heard a flute playing in the distance. It could have been someone walking home to his village. Or it could have been a memory of the past reaching our minds through the veils of time. We have had too many inexplicable experiences, in our wanderings, to deny the existence of perceptions beyond the ordinary.

Now we had the time to appreciate Pinjore at its second level.

The Gardens are not just beautiful, they are the culmination of a long line of legendary and cultural developments that reach back into the epic era of the *Mahabharata*. According to a brochure given to us, the five Pandava brothers, heroes of the *Mahabharata* war, had come to this place on their long trek into the Himalayas. It is possible that they had visited the Bhima Devi Temple, which now lies outside the walls of the Gardens. Folklorists say that the village, served by the temple, had, probably, been named Panchpura after the Pandavas. Panchpura became Pinjore. Archaeologists, examining inscriptions, believe that Pinjore was an important place between the 9th and 13th centuries. Then it declined. Its fading glory, and its perennial spring, caught the eye of the Mughal's governor and architect, Nawab Fidai Khan.In designing this garden, Fidai Khan respected traditions that went back to the nomadic Mongol tribes. In 1206, Genghiz Khan united the savage equestrian tribes of Mongolia into a conquering army: the dreaded Golden Horde. They fanned out from Mongolia and spread over Iran and Russia and then settled in China. Genghiz Khan's grandson, Kublai Khan, became the first

Pinjore Gardens framed in a scalloped Rajasthani arch.

emperor of China's Yuan Dynasty in 1279. The reputation of his splendid court spread as far as Europe's Danube River. Clearly, contact with older civilisations had mellowed these tough warriors and given them a taste for leisure. Gardens expressed their new love for a settled life and they passed it on, through their world-spanning diaspora.

Babur, a descendant of Genghiz Khan, was born in Ferghana in Central Asia. He established the Mughal Dynasty of India in 1526. Historians now believe that he also designed the first Mughal Garden. His Aram Bagh, in Agra, was almost forgotten till Indian archaeologists began to conserve, and restore, it in the late 20th century. Consequently, the claim made by the state authorities of Haryana that the Pinjore Gardens are the oldest *surviving* Mughal Gardens are correct. Thanks to the sensitivity of successive rulers of this area, including the Maharajas of Patiala, the Pinjore Gardens are, essentially, unchanged since Nawab Fidai Khan created them.

And they still express all the features typical of such Islamic gardens, ranging from those we have seen in Spain's Generalife in Cordoba to Turkey's Topkapi in Istanbul.

As a people who had been nurtured in flat, fairly featureless, lands, the Mongol-Mughal concept of Paradise was a fragrant garden, rich with fruit and flowers, cooled by sparkling streams, and enclosed in a wall to exclude harsh, abrasive winds. They liked the sound of flowing water and they built chutes into their gardens, inspired by their irrigation channels, and lined them with pebbles to make the water foam and chortle. Because water was in short supply, the pools and water courses were shallow but they were given the illusion of depth by lining them with blue ceramic tiles like the reflection of a clear sky. And if there was a distant view of rising, mountains...ah!...That would be heaven! For a desert dweller, Paradise had to be a cool, high, place.

From our window in the Sheesh Mahal we identified all these features in Pinjore, but the creative Fidai Khan had gone beyond the textbook version of Mughal Gardens. In typical Mughal Gardens, buildings played a superficial role. Even though they were permanent they had a light and rather inconsequential look: much like tents pitched, haphazardly, in a hunting park. Fidai Khan decided to break this tradition. He wanted his garden to be enjoyed by select visitors who had the option of living in it and appreciating it in the quiet hours. But he had no precedence on which to base his design for such garden apartments. Innovatively, he went beyond the Mughal-Islamic tradition. He chose a garden-apartment idiom from another, aesthetic, desert culture: that of the princely Rajputs of Rajasthan. Moreover, in the manner of Rajasthan's Sisodia Rani Bagh, the gardens slope down from the entrance and not, as the other Mughal Gardens do, rise up from the gateway. This gives Pinjore, viewed from the Sheesh Mahal, a sense of lightness, of the freedom to unwind effortlessly, high above it all.

And that...with our renewed thanks to Fidai Khan...is exactly what we did.

Shrine of the Blue Knights

ANANDPUR SAHIB

This is where our newest religion was given its iconic character, 300 years ago.

At first glance, however, Anandpur Sahib looked like just another rural township set in a fertile valley. The only unusual feature was the number of elegant Sikh shrines dotted around, particularly the imposing Keshgarh Sahib. It crowned a hillock like a proud, white, fortress of faith. With cupolas, battlements, turrets, arched windows and colonnades it had all the features of a castle but there was a grace about it that gave us the impression that it was the stronghold of a prelate rather than that of a prince.

The lesser gurdwaras stood out against the patchwork of fields, the clasping curve of the rivulet Charan Ganga, and a backdrop of low, scrubby hills.

We drove up to the entrance of Keshgarh Sahib and then, after washing our hands and feet and covering our heads with scarves, we walked into the great gurdwara. As in all gurdwaras, it was immaculately clean and the

A shield captures the martial facet of Anandpur Sahib.

sanctum enshrined the holy Guru Granth Sahib. One of the employees of the shrine, who accompanied us, said, "In its printed form the Adi Granth's 5,894 verses are always contained in exactly 1,430 pages." We knew that the last of the ten gurus of the Sikhs, Guru Gobind Singh, had decreed that this revered book would be the eternal guru after him.

He had also been responsible for a number of other prominent features of the Sikh religion. It was he who had laid out the five obligatory k's: the *kesh*, uncut hair; the *kara*, metal bracelet; the *kanghi*, comb to dress the hair; the *kirpan*, sword; and the *kaccha*, shorts. The final version of the Guru Granth Sahib was also compiled by Guru Gobind Singh. And the choice of Anandpur Sahib as the prime base of the

The revered shrine of Anandpur Sahib.

Sikhs was his: it had rich agricultural land that could feed the settlement and also had the natural barriers of rivers and mountains. The guru, besides being a man of letters, was an inspired military strategist.

Displayed on a platform, and treated with great respect, were twelve weapons once used by Guru Gobind Singh, including six that had been taken away to England by the British when they had ruled India. These had been returned after Independence.

We paused a long time, gazing at this display, while the guide explained the significance of each weapon and its association with the evolution of the Sikh way of life. The *khanda,* or double-edged sword, was the one that had been used by Guru Gobind Singh to anoint five fearless Sikhs as Khalsa, sometimes interpreted as 'sovereign beings', and endowed them with the Rajput title of Singh or lion. The gun is believed to have been presented to the Guru when he called upon Sikhs to bring him good horses, weapons and books to equip the army he needed to fight against the enemies of his people. The *naagani barchha,* the snake-shaped spear, was the weapon that had wounded the drunken elephant sent to batter down the gate of the Sikh's arsenal at Lohargarh on 1 September 1700.

We listened to these tales with growing amazement. This was the first time that we had visited the shrine of a major religion where arms had been displayed as a matter of honour. Today, however, we can appreciate the

Nihangs, guardians of the Sikh faith.

Guru Nanak journeyed to the centres of Hinduism, Islam and Buddhism in Tibet seeking to identify the Path. He found the Sufi creed of personal experience attractive, and he expressed many of his teachings in aphorisms, poetry and songs. These, eventually became part of the Sikh's holy book, the Guru Granth Sahib.

relevance of this display. We now know how a succession of ten inspired leaders changed a meek and subjugated people into a dedicated and clearly identifiable martial community, prepared to sacrifice themselves to oppose tyranny. It is a tale of the most astonishing social transformation. And it was brought about in an age when mass communication was a matter of personal charisma and word of mouth.

In those days, the Mughals ruled India and their will was law. Their emperor Aurangzeb was determined to convert all non-Muslims to his faith. He not only imposed a head tax on all he considered outside his religion, he also persecuted them as oppressively as he could. Or so one group of historians would have us believe.

For a while his down-trodden subjects accepted this. They hid from his religious police, or pretended to be converts. But, after a while, a reaction set in and a leader who would oppose Mughal rule was born.

A man born a Hindu had had a spiritual experience when he was thirty. He had said that:

'There is neither Hindu nor Mussulman so whose path should I follow?
I shall follow God's path. God is neither Hindu nor Mussulman and the Path which I follow is God's.'

Nanak is recognised as the first Guru of the Sikhs. The word 'Sikh' comes from the Sanskrit *sishya,* which is a student or disciple: one who seeks knowledge.

Nanak's successors elaborated on his message of equality, social action and monotheism. Finally, the last Guru, Gobind Singh, took up arms against his oppressors and created a Sikh army.

Though the formal army of the Guru no longer exists, the martial spirit that he engendered amongst his people has been embodied in the fiercely independent Nihangs. We have seen these bearded knights in their blue shirts, tall yellow-and-blue turbans festooned with chains and metal quoits, and armed with swords and spears, all over our land, but particularly in the gurdwaras. They act as voluntary guardians of their shrines.

Sometimes they travel with a favourite companion: a horse. We have an old clipping from the *Indian Express* dated the 20 May 1980 that brings out a Nihang's love of his independence and his mare.

Nihang Puran Singh boarded a second-class compartment in the Nangal Express along with his mount. He didn't buy a ticket either for himself or his horse. When produced before a startled magistrate, he claimed that it was his divine right, and that of his mare, to travel free on the railways. He was jailed and his mount sent to the cattle pound till a committee of Sikhs paid his fine and united the bearded blue knight with his steed.

This may sound like a quixotic tale but, then, so would the legends of derring-do undertaken by King Arthur's Knights of the Round Table. Like those selfless warriors, the Nihangs are not a burden on society: they are a yeomanry with their own fields and farms probably maintained by their families. But, as Nihangs, they should have no ties to family or property. Their military orders probably originated in the 17th century as units of fanatical, possibly suicidal, fighters.

And they still practice their martial arts.

The day after the festival of Holi, many Nihangs gather in Anandpur Sahib for the famed *Hola Mohalla*. They are grouped in camps under their leaders. Here, on the field of combat, with drums, bands and pennants flying, they display their fighting skills including tent-pegging, using specialised weapons, riding and mock battles, to the delight of cheering crowds. The *Hola Mohalla* was started by Guru Gobind Singh to hone the fighting skills of his soldiers as well as to preserve the traditional ballads and poetry of his people. From all accounts, it is the nearest our world can offer to the authentic action and chivalry of a medieval tournament.

Sadly, we have never witnessed this vibrant spectacle, capturing the martial heritage of a 300-year old faith. Which, of course, gives us something to look forward to...

Tales and Traders of the Highway of Moonlight

CHANDNI CHOWK

We have now felt the heartbeat of Delhi, the throbbing pulse of north India.

From the disciplined gardens and grounds of our club in the cantonment, the military area of Delhi, we had crouched in an auto-rickshaw and *put-putted* through broad avenues and past the imperial, red-sandstone, assertions of Lutyens New Delhi.

We'd jounced and honked our way through growling traffic. Old walls began to rise, the streets were congested and we wove and jinked with hair-raising dexterity, spun around a stone arch, hoary with age. We were in Shahjahanabad, the walled city of the Mughals.

The charitable Birds Hospital, run by the Jains.

On our right was a glacis, a stretch of unobstructed greensward for troops to repel attackers. Beyond rose Emperor Shah Jahan's massive Red Fort, the military and administrative command of a vast Indian empire. But it lacked something: a great trading centre, a bazaar to receive the wealth of the world, a place where camels from Kabul, carts from Coromandel, and the purveyors of silks and satins, spices, perfumes and gems could fill the shops of a great *souk* with the riches of an empire, and its neighbours. An imperial capital attracts traders from the far corners of the earth.

Stretching away from the main portal of the Fort, a broad thoroughfare grew. Running down its centre was a long, reflecting pool. On both sides of this road rose the huge bazaar of the Mughals. Admiring her creation, from the jasmine-scented gardens of her father's Fort, Jahanara was inspired by the silvery reflections of the lights of the *souk,* shimmering in the long pool. She decided to call the broad road 'The Highway of Moonlight': Chandni Chowk.

The year was 1648. Today, many centuries later, the reflecting pool has gone, shouldered aside by the press of traffic and traders. Chandni Chowk now refers to the labyrinth of streets and lanes and shops and religious shrines crowded together in this teeming heart of old Delhi. We wanted to see how this vibrant place had evolved over the years.

Bustling Chandni Chowk: the changed face of the Highway of Moonlight.

The Emperor's favourite daughter, Jahanara Begum, decided to build such a commercial hub. And so, it became a reality.

We left our auto in front of a sprawling, brick-red, Jain Temple. Or, to give it its official title, the Shree Digamba Jain Mandir Ji. The deep reverence that the Jains have for all life has prompted them to establish their famed Birds Hospital here. All injured birds brought to them are treated till they are fit to fly again. They are then released to live free. When we'd asked one of their doctors, "Where do you free them?" he'd pointed to a hatch opening to the blue sky. "We have to be careful when we open that hatch," he had said. "The birds are so happy here that they bring their wild companions in!"

Stepping out of this bird haven we merged with the crowds pouring into Chandni Chowk.

From the day it was created, Chandni Chowk has surged and shouted, laughed and shrieked and moaned with the changing tides of Delhi's history. The camels from Kabul have gone, the elephants of the nobles no longer sway ponderously past, but the bullock-carts still creak and joggle as they did then. Now, however, they have to compete with scooters, cars, goods vans, and hand-carts: unwieldy wooden platforms on wheels drawn by wiry, sweating, men.

Traditions fade slowly in the Chowk, and myths and memories are passed down the generations of traders sipping tea and nibbling snacks from the *halwai* next door. At least one of these confectioners is from the Himalayas and he offers pan-Indian fare: *pao-bhaji* from the West, *chhole-batura* from the North, and *dosa* from the South: his menu-board specifies South Indian just in case you don't know! And while the traders chew and recall the stories their forefathers told them, sometimes they shudder.

They recall, with horror, the time that the fanatical Emperor Aurangzeb was enraged by the growing popularity of the Sikh leader, Guru Tegh Bahadur. Aurangzeb wanted him to recant or be executed. The guru refused to change his views. The bigoted emperor had had him publicly beheaded under a banyan tree in the Chowk. Then the traders point to the soaring memorial to this great act of self-sacrifice: Gurdwara Sisganj.

We noticed crowds, hurrying along the sidewalks of Chandni Chowk, step aside as they come to the stairs leading to the shrine. Some nodded in deference, others covered their heads in reverence. A group of Caucasians washed their feet in an enclosure off the road, before entering the gurdwara. Their tour leader said, "We're in time to dine in their *langar*. Anyone can have a meal there, free of charge, and the food is good and very hygienic. But we'll all have to sit in a line, on the floor, showing that we are all equal."

We walked on.

A little further ahead schoolgirls in uniform waited in six cycle-rickshaws, shopping for peanut-brittle from the trestle table of Dharam Vir. He had come all the way from the regal city of Gwalior in Madhya Pradesh and his peanut brittle was excellent. Other girls stood around Mahavir Prasad, baking sweet potatoes in a cast-iron pan, glowing with charcoal embers. When the charred skin of a sweet potato is peeled off, the slightly yellow flesh is floury and delicious.

A girl saw us clicking our cameras and asked, in English, "You have eaten *shakarkand*?"

We said we had and we liked it very much.

She held out a leaf plate with a smoking sweet potato on it. "Have some. I have not touched it."

We thanked her and said we had just had breakfast.

She smiled a little disbelievingly and then said, "Bye!"

In brightly-lit establishments across the road, Haldirams sold packaged nibbles, McDonalds offered fast food. We wondered if Dharam Vir and Mahavir Prasad, or their descendants, would ever rise to 'DV Nibbles—the real flavour of Chandni Chowk' and 'Mahavirbakes—sweet spuds the way Grandpa made'.

But then we recalled another moment of history which brought us rudely down to earth...Chandni Chowk has had its day of mindless savagery.

In 1739, the wealth of the crumbling Mughal Empire had tempted the Turkoman usurper Nadir Shah. He had led his fearsome Persian army into Delhi on 9 March, and occupied the Red Fort. The next day, spurred by a false rumour that Nadir Shah had died, people had streamed out from Chandni Chowk, stormed the Red Fort, and attacked the Persian soldiers. To their dismay, Nadir Shah had confronted them. Burning with cold anger, he had ordered his troops to hack a path for him through the sullen crowds. Silently, he rode down the water-rippling thoroughfare and mounted the steps of a mosque with copper domes near the square of the Highway of Moonlight. He had paused a moment, looking at his vengeful troops, men who had raped and pillaged and fought with him all across the wild lands of West Asia. He looked at the shops brimming with wealth, the jewellers, the women in their bright costumes. And then he smiled. And with a deliberate plunge and sweep of his hand, he had bared his sword and held it aloft, glistening and vicious in the sun. A roar tore from the throats of his men and then it was drowned in the shrieks of the women, the cries of the children, the yells of the men as the massacre and ravaging and sacking of Chandni Chowk and Delhi began.

The slaughter had lasted for the whole day and the central channel of Chandni Chowk had run red with blood while dogs and vultures and carrion crows had swooped down and gorged themselves on the dead

A trader offers festive braids for wedding outfits.

and grievously wounded. Nothing so heartless had ever hit Delhi and it left a deep scar in the psyches of many generations of the people of Chandni Chowk.

But this is the stuff of history. For even after the dreadful pillaging by Nadir Shah, the theft of the Peacock Throne now installed in the Topkapi Palace in Istanbul, and that of the brilliant Koh-i-Noor diamond, now part of the Crown Jewels of Britain, even then the spirit of Chandni Chowk was not broken. The rains washed the streets and the walls, the sun bleached the rusty stains of tragedy. People picked up the shredded threads of their lives as generation after generation has done, because this is where even the most deprived can make a living, if he is willing to work.

People like Raju who sold us an exquisitely decorated hand mirror for just ten rupees. And Mohammed Laiq who carried his equipment in a small tin box and repaired cigarette lighters on the pavement outside McDonalds.

We paused and looked up and down the crowded road. Every period of North India's history had left its mark here. The old State Bank of India, once the Imperial Bank of the British, still occupied a solid, stolid, Victorian building that would have looked more comfortable in the City of London. The Baptist Church, with its tall spire, recalled the work of evangelists in North India. Back on our side of the street, Tibetan monks, clustered around an electronics store, ogling the latest Blackberries. They were the last ethnic group to seek sanctuary in India, fleeing persecution on the Roof of the World.

Chandni Chowk has always welcomed the migrant from other lands, other places. Bali Ram, the flower-seller, displays his blossoms in baskets on the pavement, Ankit Gupta perches in his open-fronted shop in Kinari

The original eatery in Gali Paranthe Wali.

Bazaar. This is the street of dreams. It glitters with festoons of wedding decorations enriched with gold and silver *zari* thread. Here, Indian grooms are enrobed as princes, with all the regalia of royalty even if much of it is make-believe. A mother and sister examined the glitter very carefully, seeking to give *A Suitable Boy* the most convincing of royal illusions. He could well be a software engineer with a Harvard accent but when he meets his bride around the sacred fire, he is a Vedic Prince-for-a-Day.

We made our way to an even more famous landmark: Gali Paranthe Wali, 'The Alley of the Unleavened Breads'. High old houses towered on both sides, making a canyon with only a glimpse of the sky above. The air was heavy with frying flavours: the sizzle of ghee, the bite of chillies, the rasp of onions browning, the tang of herbal sauces. Diners sat around small tables, packed tightly, lights hazed by the aromatic blue smoke from the sizzling pans.

Down the lane, other *paranthe wallas* created their own versions of this stalwart dish. While a traditional *maharaj* cook from Uttar Pradesh presided over the kitchen, the owner of Pt. Gaya Prasad Shiv Charan restaurant sat at a desk at the entrance, punched out bills on an electronic calculator, and flipped the cash into a drawer. He told us that he was the sixth generation of his family to run this restaurant, his son would be the seventh, and that all the other *paranthe* eating houses on the *gali* were owned by his relatives. His ancestor had come from Madhya Pradesh.

"Are you worried about competition from the other establishments?" we asked.

He probably didn't hear but a customer, paying his bill, turned to us and said, "Here in the Chowk, for 400 years, there has always been enough for everyone who is willing to adjust..."

The Tibetan monks walked past us, chatting. Then they merged, indistinguishable in the busy mélange of Chandni Chowk.

About the Authors

Hugh and Colleen Gantzer live their dream. Colleen had always wanted to fly and she did pilot a plane in the Swiss Alps while Hugh sat behind saying a rosary, just in case! Hugh had longed to see those faraway places with their strange sounding names so he joined the Indian Navy. Hugh took premature retirement when he was the Judge Advocate of the Southern Naval Area and Hugh and Colleen decided to become a travel-writer-photographer team.

Suddenly, things changed. They found themselves surfing on the great travel wave that was sweeping across the world. In quick succession they launched India's first travel column carried in all editions of a national daily on the editorial page. They hosted fifty-two weekly episodes of India's first nation-wide TV travel show, wrote the first travel scripts for dot.coms, won national and international awards, toured India and the world as guests of eager tourism organisations. They have, possibly, visited, photographed and written about more places in India than anyone else in the long history of our land.

Once, a greatly revered maternal uncle, who had just retired as India's Naval Chief, had asked them, "How long more will you continue to travel?" That was before they were invited to a winter ball in Vienna. Today, for six months every year, when they're not in their Victorian cottage in the oak woods of the Himalayas, they're still travelling...and they're still having a ball.

Other Books in
the Intriguing India Series

The
Colourful
East

The
Vibrant

West

The
Historic
South